Learning to Cook

Marguerite Patten began her career as a demonstrator with a fuel company and, during the war, worked as a senior demonstrator with the Ministry of Food, showing women how to keep their families fit on the available rations. From 1943–50 she was responsible for the Food Advice and Home Service Advice Bureau at Harrods. During this time, she was invited to broadcast on early morning household and cooking programmes and began regular BBC TV cookery programmes in 1947. When in 1956, BBC TV started their Cookery Club, Marguerite Patten became President, and for five years viewers sent in recipes which she tested on television. She demonstrates and gives lectures throughout Britain and has also worked on Australian television. She now writes regularly for *Woman's Own* and has had over sixty cookery books published.

Marguerite Patten lives in Brighton with her husband, and has one daughter.

Other cookery books available in Pan

Mrs Beeton
All About Cookery

Ada Boni
The Talisman Italian Cook Book

Lousene Rousseau Brunner
New Casserole Treasury

Savitri Chowdhary
Indian Cooking

Theodore FitzGibbon
A Taste of Ireland
A Taste of London
A Taste of Scotland
A Taste of Wales
A Taste of the West Country

Dorothy Hall
The Book of Herbs

Robin Howe
Soups

Rosemary Hume and Muriel Downes
The Cordon Bleu Book of Jams, Preserves and Pickles

Kenneth Lo
Quick and Easy Chinese Cooking

Claire Loewenfeld and Philippa Back
Herbs for Health and Cookery

R. J. Minney (ed.)
The George Bernard Shaw Vegetarian Cook Book

Jennie Reekie
Traditional French Cooking

Constance Spry and Rosemary Hume
The Constance Spry Cookery Book

Katie Stewart
The Times Cookery Book

Marika Hanbury Tenison
Eat Well and Be Slim
Deep-Freeze Cookery
Deep-Freeze Sense

Marguerite Patten

Learning to Cook

Pan Books London and Sydney

First published 1955 by J. M. Dent & Sons Ltd
Published 1958 by Pan Books Ltd, and
reprinted 1963
This revised edition published 1972 by
Pan Books Ltd, Cavaye Place, London SW10 9PG
Reprinted 1974, 1976
© Marguerite Patten 1972
ISBN 0 330 23025 5
Printed and bound in Great Britain by
Richard Clay (The Chaucer Press) Ltd, Bungay, Suffolk

CONTENTS

SECTION IV

ILLUSTRATIONS IN PHOTOGRAVURE

Introduction

While this book is primarily intended for the new, and therefore less experienced, housewife, it contains many recipes which I think you will like to continue to use as you become more and more expert.

The first section will help you to equip your kitchen both practically and economically, will give you information about the various types of cookers available, and will help you to have a sensibly filled store cupboard. In this section also are tables showing how to choose, cook, and serve Meat, Poultry, Game, Vegetables, and Fish.

In the second section you will find explanations of the specialized terms used in cookery, hints on using left-overs, how to turn what seems a failure into a success, and the quantities to allow when shopping. Section III contains a monthly calendar of foods in season, so that you can see very quickly which foods are cheapest and best to buy; then come instructions for preparing these foods. The main meal of the day often seems frightening to the new cook, so in each case I have given a 'Plan of Work', and if you follow this the meal will be ready with the least amount of fuss and bother. Christmas catering and menus for special occasions also come into this section.

Throughout the book I have given directions for cooking as easily and economically as possible, not only by using economical ingredients but by using fuel wisely. In many meals you will find I use the oven entirely, in others the top part of the cooker, the oven not being in use at all, or put at a very low heat, which uses little fuel. I would, however, especially like to draw your attention to the three fuel-saving plans in Section III, which give menus for an oven-cooked meal, a meal cooked in a steamer, or on the grill. These suggestions will help you to save both time and money.

In the last section of the book you will find directions for making jam and bottling fruit.

Section I

Choosing kitchen equipment. Choosing your cooker. Special cookers. Filling your store cupboard. Herbs to improve your cooking. Choosing meat, poultry, game. To cook and serve vegetables. Choosing fish

---

Choosing Kitchen Equipment

There is one wise rule when choosing kitchen equipment, particularly the type of equipment you will use day after day – saucepans, the cooker, etc; buy the best you can afford, for it will repay you in years of efficient service.

I have listed some of the things you will need to buy when you first equip your kitchen. To some people it may seem a short list, but remember that it does not include cake-making equipment, although you will doubtless find that some of the utensils I give below can also be extremely useful when you are making cakes.

Hints on choosing a cooker are on page 18, so they are not included here.

Baking tins. You will need about two flat baking trays of the size to fit comfortably in your oven for baking patties, etc. When you choose these, make sure they are not so large that they come right over the heating elements, otherwise the food at the edges will burn.

Always wipe these very dry after you have washed them, and leave in a warm place for an hour or so before putting into the cupboard.

Basins and bowl. You will need one good-sized mixing bowl, not less than 4–5 pints capacity, for pastry and cakes, for a too small bowl hinders movement. You will need about 3 basins, approximately 1, 1½, and 2 pints in capacity – either china or oven- and heat-proof glassware.

11

Boards. Even if you use the top of an enamel or Formica table for rolling out pastry, etc, you will find a small board essential for chopping and cutting.

Always wash the board in warm – not too hot – water. Dry with a cloth, then store in a warm place for a little time before you put it into the cupboard.

With a plain wooden table you may like to have a small Formica or enamel pastry board; because it is so cool it does assist in making good pastry.

Brushes. You will need at least one small pastry brush; since they are not expensive you may like to have two. Use one for greasing tins (a small quantity of fat for this purpose can be stored in a tiny basin, old cup, or earthenware jar and heated over a pan of boiling water). The second brush should then be kept for brushing pies, etc, with egg, milk. Choose good quality brushes, of pure bristle if possible.

Wash the brushes in warm soapy water. Rinse in plenty of clean water.

Casseroles. Casserole cookery is very popular and you will find use for several casseroles. If possible select those with lids which form a separate cooking utensil; oven-proof glassware is particularly sensible. Oval and rectangular casseroles take up less room in the oven than round ones, but it is not always so easy to arrange food in them. You will find casseroles easier to remove from the oven if you stand them on a metal baking tray; you can then pull out the whole tray.

Castle pudding tins. *See* Moulds.

Colander. Essential for draining and straining vegetables. It can be used as an emergency steamer.

Cutters. While the tops of glasses, etc, can be used for cutting rounds of pastry, a much more professional appearance is given by using proper metal cutters. All shapes and sizes can be obtained.

Wash and dry as for metal baking trays.

Dredgers. If possible have two of these – one for flour (essential when rolling out pastry), and one for sugar. They can be of china or metal, and it is quite easy to improvise with old tins, pierced with small holes.

Fish slice. Essential for lifting and supporting food, and for draining away surplus fat. It is worthwhile having two slices, a light pliable one for lifting fairly solid foods such as fritters, and one of firmer construction to support eggs and fish.

Forks. Have one or two kitchen forks for mashing vegetables, sealing edges of pastry, etc.

Frying-pans. Choose the heaviest one you can afford, for frying needs high temperatures and cheap, light pans quickly become uneven. After washing the pan dry it well, for this makes a great deal of difference to the success of future frying.

Even if you grill most foods, you will need an *omelet pan* for pancakes and omelets. This should never be washed; wipe it out *immediately* after use with crumpled tissue paper. Buy a small pan with rounded edges for easy cleaning.

As explained on page 46 frying in a pan of deep fat is more successful. A deep fryer consists of a pan rather like a saucepan with a wire basket that allows you to lower the food into and withdraw it from the hot fat. With care you need never turn the fat out of the fryer, cleaning it as explained on page 118. For economy's sake you could buy a frying basket for a few shillings to fit inside an ordinary saucepan.

Grater. Some kind of grater is essential, and I would choose one with holes of several sizes for grating lemon rind, cheese, etc.

Wash with a small scrubbing brush to make sure you have cleaned all the holes, and dry in a warm place before putting it away.

Kettle. You must have some form of kettle, and do choose one of sufficient capacity, for a large kettle can always be half filled, but it is most annoying to wait for two lots of water. For a gas cooker buy light aluminium (which, while more expensive, wears best), enamel, or light tin. For an electric cooker, if you have no electric kettle, a heavier one is advisable with solid plates; a lighter one will do for radiant plates. Always cover the hotplate so that no heat is wasted.

Look for a kettle with a heat-resistant handle and a good-sized lid for easy filling. See that there is a vent for the steam, and the lid does not fall off when pouring.

Knives. A good selection of knives is essential. You will need: *Carving knife:* as sharp as possible, and have two if you can, for the heat of meat blunts the edge after carving for two or three people. *Kitchen knife:* perhaps two for general purposes. *Palette knife:* one of the most useful pieces of equipment for turning out pancakes, lifting food out of pans, cleaning out basins, etc. *Sharp knife:* essential to have one at least for cutting and chopping. *Small vegetable knife:* for preparing fruit, vegetables, etc.

Stainless steel knives are much sharper now than they used to be. Handle several patterns to find what suits your hand best, but do have one with a rigid blade for spreading butter, etc.

A *potato peeler* is not essential but helps a great deal. There are a number of designs available; handle them in the shop before buying.

Meat tin or Roasting tin. Generally supplied with the cooker, for roasting meat. You may be interested in the covered self-basting tins that stop splashing of fat in the oven.

Mincer. When you begin to do more cooking you will find a mincer of some kind very useful for making good use of left-over meat, etc. Models available range from mincing attachments for electric mixers to quite cheap hand models; buy the best you can afford. A reasonably heavy mincer will stand without being screwed to a table. If you choose the screw-on type make sure the nuts are insulated so that there is no fear of cracking enamel surfaces. Choose a stainless-bladed model. For very fine shredding the Mouli shredder or grater is excellent; the food is passed through quickly and easily and it produces almost a purée.

Wash and dry the mincer most carefully and stand it near the cooker to dry thoroughly.

Moulds. Although you can use basins for setting jellies, etc, one or two attractively shaped moulds do assist in making your dishes look interesting. Many of the aluminium moulds can be used for baking cakes. Small castle pudding tins, or dariole moulds, are useful for cooking steamed puddings quickly.

Wash and dry carefully and leave in a warm place for an hour or so before putting away.

Paper. Always keep a small stock of both greaseproof and tissue paper in your kitchen cupboard, the former to line tins, wrap foods inside tins, etc, the latter for careful draining of fried foods.

Pie dishes. You can use the bottoms of oval casseroles, provided they have a good rim, for pies. Have at least two sizes – 1½ and 2 pints approximately.

Pie support. This keeps a meat or fruit pie a good shape. An egg cup make a good substitute.

Rolling pin. The modern glass or china rolling pins, while more fragile than wooden ones, are popular because they keep pastry cool and they are easy to handle and to clean. If your rolling pin is wooden look after it in the same way as the board.

Sauceboat. An oven-proof glassware sauceboat is a useful extra for keeping sauces hot, since most dinner services seem to provide only one boat.

Saucepans. The number you have depends very much on the amount of cooking you intend to do. If you are fond of sauces, then you *must* have extra pans or you will find yourself seriously inconvenienced.

Remember to choose pans with heavy bases if you have an electric or solid fuel cooker. In any case, a reasonably heavy pan is always a good investment, for it lasts for years.

You will need a small pan for small quantities of milk – look out for the patent milk saucepans with centre device to stop milk boiling over; two saucepans for vegetables, approximately 4–5 pints capacity; a large pan for boiling pieces of beef, ham, etc; and one that could be used for jam-making in small quantities. This should be large enough for the jam to boil without boiling over, minimum capacity 8 pints. Enamel, provided it is not chipped, and aluminium are ideal for jam-making, though I prefer the latter.

A *double saucepan* is an ideal way of making porridge, and keeping custards and sauces hot without fear of burning. Both parts can generally be used as separate pans when desired.

Scales. Undoubtedly if you are to become a first-class cook you must invest in a pair of scales for careful measuring, although it is possible to measure by spoonfuls or cupfuls. Those with weights are inclined to give greater accuracy over a long period.

Scissors. Invest in a pair of kitchen scissors, and you will use these many times a day, for removing bacon rinds, chopping parsley, cutting salads, all much easier with scissors than with a knife.

Sieves. In a number of recipes one is told to 'sieve' the ingredients, which means push them through the mesh of a fine sieve and so produce a smooth mixture. A hair sieve is ideal for vegetables and fruits, since there is no fear of the metal discolouring the food. You also need a wire sieve to cool pastry and cakes on, and a fine wire sieve for mixing flour and baking powder or lightening flour.

Do wash and dry your sieves most carefully, for the hair mesh will rot if left damp, and the metal ones may rust.

Spoons. As well as the ordinary kitchen metal spoons, you will need about two wooden spoons. Get in the habit of using *wooden* spoons when you stir sauces, for they give a far better movement, and are therefore less likely to allow the sauce or soup to become lumpy. Wash and dry like wooden boards.

You may prefer to measure dry ingredients in a spoon, in which case make sure you have the proper measuring spoons, made in plastic and conforming to the British Standard Institution's recommendations. Throughout this book spoon measures (as all others) are based on the BSI measure and are *level* spoonfuls, unless otherwise stated. You can also obtain a BSI measuring cup which, to a great extent, takes the place of scales.

Squeezer. A lemon squeezer for extracting juice from citrus fruits is very important. Clean with a small brush.

Steamer. Although you can manage without a steamer in your kitchen, it is a most useful cooking utensil, enabling you to cook several dishes on one plate or ring, and giving very light puddings. If you buy a one-tier steamer, choose a pattern to which you can add a second and perhaps even a third tier later.

Keep your steamer – like your saucepans – clean by careful washing immediately after use.

DON'T USE SODA ON ANY ALUMINIUM COOKING UTENSILS

Storage jars, etc. You must plan a certain amount of storage equipment, ie, tins for cakes, biscuits, and pastry, which must all be kept separately. Bread can be stored in a bread bin, or wrapped in a cloth and put into a drawer with a certain amount of air circulation. There are most attractive sets of tins or jars for storing all dry goods, and these save time by indicating at once the contents of the jar or tin.

Strainer. You will need a small strainer for coffee and tea, and this would also be handy for straining any small lumps from a sauce, should they occur. When you can, buy a larger strainer suitable for straining stocks, etc.

Tin opener. Choose a strong one that will open most types of tins – that is, the lever type. Also buy a master 'key' for sardine tins, since the small ones supplied so often break or get lost.

Tongs. You can now buy kitchen 'tongs' which are extremely useful for picking up foods either too delicate to handle or too hot.

Vegetable brush. A small brush is invaluable for cleaning vegetables.

Whisk. An egg whisk of some kind is essential for beating egg whites quickly and easily, although some people like to beat the egg whites on a flat plate or dish with a palette knife. There are a number of whisks on the market – varying in design and price. Handle them, so that you have an idea which one feels the most comfortable to use.
Wash and dry the whisk very well before putting away.

Yorkshire pudding tin, etc. A square metal tin is useful for baking Yorkshire puddings (*see* p 86). *Round flan rings* are also a useful utensil, for the pastry is easily removed from the tin so lessening the chances of its breaking. Clean and store carefully as all metal tins.

These are the basic utensils in your kitchen. Keep them in useful places; whisks and fish slices are best hung on plastic hooks, so that they are easy to pick up. There will be many other utensils you can add from time to time, varying a great deal in price, of course.

An electric mixer – of which there are many on the market – does all your mincing, beating, and sieving by electricity, and is therefore invaluable to the busy cook.

17

There are utensils designed to cut pastry, to mash vegetables, to slice eggs, and so on, but you can manage without them when first furnishing your kitchen.

Old cups and saucers (providing they are not badly chipped) will always find a useful place in the kitchen for holding small quantities of things, like chopped parsley, or instead of small basins.

Buy one or two glass plates that can be used not only for baking pies and for serving them on as well, but for arranging salads, etc, on the table.

Save old mayonnaise bottles to store your own home-made mayonnaise or French dressing in.

Choosing your Cooker

It is wise to give careful thought to your choice of cooker, for it has to last for some years, and can make or mar your cooking.

Electric cooker. Modern electric cookers are attractive to look at. They have simmering devices that enable you to control the heat of plates and grill most easily. The radiant type boiling plates allow one to use lighter types of saucepans, while still being able to have three saucepans boiling on one plate. These plates are quick to heat up. The griller boiler is a popular feature of electric cookers, for one can cook a complete meal on the one plate, three pans above, steak, etc, underneath, in a very short time (*see* p 189). In the oven you can be sure of easily controlled heat, for the thermostat enables you to get exactly the temperature required. Modern cookers have a heated warming drawer for plates and dishes and an automatic device which enables you to leave the cooker to switch itself on for cooking and off when the meal is ready.

Cleaning is easily done. From most cookers you can take out the oven interior and all that is necessary is to wash it in warm soapy water, preferably while it is warm from cooking. The heating elements – both solid and quick-boiling radiant plates – remove easily, so that the entire hob can be cleaned within a matter of minutes.

The small diagram opposite shows the relative heats in parts of most electric cookers, but be guided by the manufacturer's instructions.

HOTTEST PART.	For Yorkshire pudding, small tarts, cakes, etc.
COOLEST PART.	Ideal for puddings, casseroles.
HOT PART.	Put meat tin on bottom or near bottom.

Gas cooker. Illustrated you will find one of the most modern gas cookers.

Practically all modern gas cookers have a pilot light which enables the gas rings to ignite at the touch of a tap. The heat is easily controlled for rapid boiling or simmering. One new model has an eye-level grill, which stops any bending down to see if food is cooked. The oven is delightfully easy to keep clean, and with the thermostat setting provides perfect control of oven temperatures.

The enamel needs just a wipe with a soapy cloth, preferably while the stove is hot. The oven shelves come out and can again be washed in warm soapy water. The tops of the hobs all remove, and these should be wiped and dried.

The small diagram below shows relative heats in parts of the cooker, but be guided by the manufacturer's instructions.

HOTTEST PART.	For Yorkshire puddings, small tarts, cakes, etc.
NEXT HOTTEST PART.	For meat.
COOLEST PART.	For puddings, casseroles.

Solid fuel cooker. These cookers have the advantage of singular economy in running costs, and the fact that heat is always available. A typical model has ample boiling capacity on top and two ovens, the lower one for slow simmering and the top one for roasting and baking. Solid fuel cookers are famous for good uniform heating, and give excellent results, both for slow cooking – which has an admirable flavour – and for cake-making or meat-roasting. The thermostat provides easy control of the heat. Always be guided by the manufacturer's instructions.

The modern solid fuel cooker is perfectly easy to keep clean, with its attractive cream and black enamel.

Oil cooker. Modern cooking by oil is thoroughly up-to-date and economical. The heat can be regulated at will by easy control of the wick to ensure correct heat and oven temperature. The cookers are table high, portable, and can be placed practically anywhere without trouble or fixing. The ovens are fitted with glass windows.

They are easy to keep clean, the enamelled surface requiring only a wipe with a warm soapy cloth. The burners must be cleaned and the lamps trimmed after use, otherwise the next batch of cooking may be spoilt by fumes and smoke. Follow carefully the instructions which are supplied by the manufacturers with all cookers.

These, then, are the main types of cookers. I suggest that whenever possible you attend cooking demonstrations so that you can choose the cooker that will be the most economical and efficient for *you*.

Special Cookers

Pressure cooker. During recent years small convenient pressure cookers have been widely demonstrated and have proved invaluable to busy housewives. They can be used on any stove – gas, electric, solid fuel, oil – where you can control the heat.

The principle is easy to understand. Because a pressure cooker is completely airtight during the process of cooking, steam cannot escape, and it therefore builds up inside the pan and produces extremely high temperatures and pressure. This means one can cook foods in an incredibly short time, and with great success. In my opinion a pressure cooker is a wise investment, for obviously if you shorten cooking time you must save a great deal of fuel.

The best uses of a pressure cooker are for:

Soups and stocks, when cooking time is shortened to about a quarter of the ordinary time;

Stews, when you produce a stew in about 20 minutes;

Vegetables, root vegetables, about 5–8 minutes, green vegetables, 1–3 minutes.

All pressure cooker manufacturers supply an instruction book, and, if wished, the recipes in this book, too, can easily be used with your pressure cooker when you have learnt how to handle this. Don't imagine, though, that pressure cookers will entirely take the place of ordinary boiling, braising, and roasting, for that is far from true. Experienced housewives find they learn to be discerning about the times when and when not to use a pressure cooker.

Electric toaster grill. This useful type of appliance is both a table toaster and grill – useful for snacks.

Electric frying-pan. This is a most elegant frying-pan which enables you to cook breakfast bacon and eggs at the table, or to prepare a variety of fried dishes. It has a thermostat so can be set to the correct heat. In addition to frying the domed lid enables you to treat it as a table casserole or small oven, etc.

Portable cooker or Wonder oven. This small cooker is excellent for people who cook on a very small stove, with restricted cooking capacity in the oven. You can efficiently bake, roast, stew, or casserole in it. It can be used on gas, oil, or portable picnic stoves – not solid fuel or electricity. It has a thermometer, which means it can be regulated for different temperatures.

For luxury picnics you can take this with an oil stove, and produce complete meals with little difficulty.

Filling your Store Cupboard

Do not run away with the idea that your pantry must be absolutely full of elaborate foods. This is not the case – the lists given here are sufficient to provide the basis for a very great number of dishes.

It is wise to keep a slate or shopping list in the kitchen, and when you are coming to the end of a food or condiment or ingredient make a note on the list, for nothing is more annoying than suddenly to run short of, say, flour or salt in the middle of cooking. The foods can roughly be divided into three groups, each requiring its own conditions of storing. These are: dry goods; perishable foods (which must be stored with particular care); preserved foods, ie, tinned food, bottled fruits, jams, and potted meat.

DRY GOODS

Although these are the easiest group of foods to store, try to see they are kept in a dry, well-ventilated pantry or store cupboard. It is advisable to store all spices in one place, condiments in another, and so on, for you save a great deal of time when cooking if you know exactly where to 'lay your hands' on a particular container.

Baking powder. You will not use this in general cooking if you buy self-raising flour. If you do buy baking powder, don't purchase too large a tin at one time, since it deteriorates very slowly with keeping. It must be kept *dry*.

Barley (pearl). This is used in some soups, such as Scotch Broth, and forms a useful and filling addition to the dish. Keeps well in dry place, but you will not use it very often, so do not buy too large a quantity; $\frac{1}{2}$ to 1 lb will be plenty.

Bicarbonate of soda. In general cooking (as opposed to cakemaking) you will need this rarely with self-raising flour. Store as baking powder.

Breadcrumbs, dried (or raspings). You can buy packets or make your own, with breadcrumbs, baking slowly in a very low oven, then rolled until very fine. You'll use them for coating fish, etc, (*see* p 117).

Cocoa or chocolate. Used to flavour puddings as well as for drinks. Keeps well in a dry place.

Coffee. You will find directions for making coffee on page 62, and, as you will see, it is essential to buy coffee fresh, for it deteriorates badly. When you open a tin or bag of coffee transfer to a covered jar. Even so, replace with fresh coffee as often as

22

possible. There are many varieties available, but you need not be concerned with more than one or two unless your ambition is to become a connoisseur. Do, however, buy the best you can afford of a particular type. Breakfast coffee is usually a lighter roast than after-dinner coffee; it is sometimes called 'American roast'. For black coffee choose the darker kind, with a richer flavour, sometimes called 'Continental roast'. If you like your coffee with a strong bite, choose one to which a little chicory has been added.

Colourings. These are not essential, but a few drops of cochineal can improve the appearance of many dishes. This deep pink colouring must be used sparingly. The best method of putting it into recipes is to drop from a skewer. Apple-green colouring is another attractive colour. These do not deteriorate if stored in a dry place.

Cornflakes (or other breakfast cereals). Keep packets tightly sealed down, for they lose their pleasant crispness if in contact with the air.

Cornflour (and blancmange). This is used for making moulds, and a little can be used in place of flour (1 oz in 4 oz) when making cakes or puddings to give a finer texture. You can use cornflour in sauces as well. The flavoured cornflours are useful for varying flavour of moulds. Store in dry place; it keeps well for a very long time.

Crystallized cherries, etc. Cherries, angelica, and peel are all useful commodities to have in the store cupboard, for they flavour cakes, puddings, sweets, and give colour to the finished dish. Keep in tins or well covered, otherwise they either go very sticky or harden.

Custard powder. For custard sauce. *See* CORNFLOUR.

Dried fruit. Currants, sultanas, raisins are all useful to keep for cakes and puddings. Since the fruit must be dry when used in baking it is a good idea to wash it the moment it arrives from the grocer. Put into a colander, and run hot water over it until clean. Spread on flat trays and dry in the warmth of the kitchen for 48 hours. Store in tins in a dry, cool place.

Other dried fruit – prunes, apricots, and so on – make an excellent change from fresh fruit (*see* pp 187–8).

Flavourings. One can buy an unlimited amount of these, both sweet and savoury, but until you are sure of those you like particularly, I would just have:

Anchovy essence, for fish sauces, etc. Marmite or Bovril, for meat dishes. Almond essence and Vanilla essence, for sweets and puddings.

Flour. If you do a great deal of baking you may prefer to have plain flour and adjust your baking powder to the particular dish you are making. But self-raising flour is excellent for most purposes, and for the beginner it does do away with the worry of how much baking powder to add, or the possibility of forgetting to add any when it is very necessary. For pastry I personally prefer plain flour, but you can make excellent short crust with self-raising. Store your flour in a dry tin or drawer. If you do little baking don't buy in large quantities.

Macaroni. *See* SPAGHETTI.

Marmite. Listed under flavourings, but it is a valuable food product.

Mustard. An essential condiment and flavouring for many savoury dishes. Most people prefer English mustard, though some like ready prepared French mustard instead. When you have mixed mustard for the table, do wash up the container frequently, for it hardens quickly, and nothing looks worse.

Oatmeal and/or Porridge Oats. Various types are described under porridge (*see* p 60). Store in a cool, dry place.

Peppers. The most useful and usual is an ordinary white pepper, which can be used for the table and cooking. If you are very fond of the flavour it is worth remembering that black pepper is stronger. *Paprika* pepper is mentioned in this book both for flavouring and garnishing the tops of dishes. This has a sweet, rather than hot, flavour and is extremely useful. A small quantity ($\frac{1}{2}$ or 1 oz) will last a very long time. It is bright red. *Cayenne* pepper, while looking very like paprika, has a very hot flavour, so use sparingly.

Rice. You will use this for savoury and sweet dishes. For curries ask for Patna rice, which is less highly polished and has longer grains than the rice suitable for milk puddings. Store in a dry place.

Salt. Refined salt can be bought in drums or packets. The former is better, since it helps to keep salt dry. It may be wise to store away from the kitchen, since steam tends to make it soft and sticky. The block kitchen salt is cheaper to buy, better for preserving, and can easily be crushed for table or kitchen use. Crushed cooking salt can also be bought.

Sauces. There is an unlimited number of made-up sauces on the market, and you will gradually discover those you like. I would have a small bottle of Worcester sauce in the store cupboard, for it is very useful in cooking.

Spaghetti (or Macaroni). Keep a small quantity in the cupboard for savoury dishes. Does not spoil easily.

Spices. As with flavourings, a long list could be made, but these are the most useful:

SAVOURY. *Curry powder*. Essential if you like curries.
SWEET. *Allspice (or Mixed Spice)*. A combination of cinnamon, ginger, and nutmeg. You can manage with a small drum of this. *Cinnamon*. For cakes and puddings. *Ginger*. Also for cakes and puddings (if you like the taste of ginger). *Nutmeg*. Buy whole nutmeg, and grate your own as you need it.

Sugar. There are several kinds of sugar. CASTOR. Best for cakes and puddings, since it has a refined texture. DEMERARA. Dry brown sugar, lovely for sweetening fruits since it gives a rich flavour. Is considered more nutritious than white sugar. A soft, sticky brown sugar, known as 'moist sugar', is also available. Either of these is recommended for rich, dark cakes and Christmas puddings. GRANULATED. The most usual for general purposes and jam-making. ICING. For decorating cakes. Has a tendency to go lumpy, so keep in airtight tin. LOAF. For table use and jam-making. PRESERVING. For jam-making.

Syrup and Treacle. GOLDEN SYRUP is an excellent sweetener and can also be used for sauces. Keeps well in dry place. BLACK

TREACLE is not so useful because of its pronounced flavour, but is an excellent source of iron.

Tea. Keeps well in a dry place. Most people prefer Indian to China tea for all occasions, but if you or regular guests like China it is worthwhile buying a little to serve with lemon instead of milk at teatime.

Vinegar. There are a number of types of vinegar with various flavours, but for general purposes buy a *good quality* malt vinegar.

PERISHABLE GOODS

These are the foods that spoil easily, and should be stored in the coolest place possible. If you have a refrigerator that is ideal for most of them. You will find hints on page 131 for taking particular care in storing these foods in very hot weather.

Bacon. Many people prefer the type of bacon known as streaky, in which lean and fat run like a ribbon along the rashers. This is a comparatively cheap cut of good flavour, and excellent for all purposes. A more expensive type of bacon is a gammon rasher, in which you generally find the fat and lean quite separate. Many people consider the flavour far better, but of course you pay considerably more per pound. The collar or back, which looks like gammon, is again a good choice; it should have a generous amount of lean. Get your grocer to show you the various pieces, and select the variety you think you will prefer, for some people like very lean bacon, others more fat. A good grocer will cut the bacon as thick or as thin as you like, and advise you whether it is mild or rather salty – again a matter of personal taste.

To store, wrap in damp cloth moistened with a little vinegar, then in greaseproof paper or container. Keep covered with paper or in dish in your refrigerator.

Cheese. There is a wide variety of cheese available; here is a selection. FOR COOKING AND TABLE. *Cheddar*. Ask for a firm cheese (ie, well matured) for easy grating. *Cheshire*. Slightly stronger than Cheddar. Excellent for cooking when firm. FOR COOKING ONLY. *Parmesan*. Hard Italian cheese with very strong flavour. Can be bought in drums ready grated. FOR TABLE USE ONLY. *Brie and Camembert*. See the cheese is soft; if it is hard it is not mature and lacks flavour. When mature it should be eaten within two days. *Blue cheese, Gorgonzola, and Stilton.* Should be slightly crumbly.

Store cheese as bacon; a lump of sugar helps to keep the harder cheese moist. Cover with vinegar-moistened cloth in your refrigerator.

Eggs. Store in cool, dry place. An egg box or rack helps to prevent cracking. They can be kept in the refrigerator if you have space. Ideally they should not be kept more than a few days; after that they should be turned daily. *Duck eggs* should always be cooked well before serving. They are better served hard-boiled, or used in cakes – never use them for meringues or icings, as there might be a slight risk of food poisoning.

Fats. BUTTER. Salted butter will keep better than fresh. You can select from Australian, Danish, English, and New Zealand brands. Unsalted butter is better for butter icings and sweet sandwiches, but choice depends on personal taste. LARD. Keeps very well. Ideal for basting and frying meat, roasting potatoes; for pastry (mixed with margarine if wished) especially for meat or savoury pies. MARGARINE. There are many brands available at different prices, so try several. Salted margarine keeps better than unsalted. The unsalted is better for cake fillings and sweet sauces. SUET. Ask for *kidney* suet. When fresh it is firm with a faintly pink tinge. Prepared shredded suet can be bought in packets; this must be freshly purchased for use or it dries and becomes rancid. VEGETABLE FATS OR SHORTENING. Can be used for cooking fish instead of oil, or in any dish where the 'meaty' flavour of lard or dripping is not desirable. In shortcrust pastry never use more than $3\frac{1}{2}$ oz to 8 oz flour, as it is very rich and causes pastry to crumble.

All fats must be kept in a cool place with plenty of air circulation. Suet should be dusted with flour to help keep it. Oil keeps well in a cool place (not necessarily the refrigerator except in very hot weather). Have a covered container for all fats in your refrigerator.

Fruit. Keep most fruit in a cool place, though it is not essential to store in the refrigerator. Bananas and melon should not be put into refrigerator except to chill at the last minute before serving.

Meat. *See* Choosing Meat, page 31. Keep *raw meat* in meat safe or covered with muslin moistened with vinegar, with good air circulation. Keep uncovered in the refrigerator. Keep *cooked meat* with great care in meat safe or covered with muslin. Keep covered in refrigerator to prevent drying.

Milk. FRESH. You may be able to buy Jersey milk, which is slightly more expensive but which has a higher fat content and more cream. In cooler weather milk will keep in a cool place with plenty of air circulation. For hot weather storage *see* p 131. TINNED. *Unsweetened evaporated* milk is a good substitute for cream in sauces, etc, if used undiluted. Diluted (as instructions on the tin), it can be substituted for milk in an emergency. *Sweetened condensed* milk can be used for the same purposes, but it is *very* sweet. Tinned milk and cream should be stored in a cool cupboard.

Vegetables. Green vegetables should be used as soon as possible after purchase. New potatoes, being immature, should be eaten within a few days. Old potatoes and other root vegetables may be kept for a week or two.

A well-ventilated vegetable rack is best for storing. Salad vegetables can be stored in a covered container in the refrigerator and things like cauliflower in plastic bags. You *must* cover them carefully. For hot-weather storage *see* p 131.

FROZEN FOODS

During recent years frozen vegetables, fruit, and ice cream have become part of our catering plans. These packets must be kept most carefully. If you have a refrigerator, store in the freezing compartment: one star marking for one week, two stars for one month, three stars for three months. To preserve in good condition for several hours without a refrigerator, wrap in thick layer of newspaper and store in the coolest place available. Follow exactly the directions on the packets for cooking or heating.

PRESERVED FOODS

Bottled fruit. Store in a cool, dry, and, if possible, dark cupboard.

Jams, chutneys. As for bottled fruit.

Potted meat and fish. These keep well until opened, if stored in a cool dry place. When opened they should be used up quickly for they become dangerous to eat if kept more than a day.

Tinned goods. Store in a cool, dry, and, if possible, dark cupboard. It is wise to have a small selection of these foods in the house, so that you are prepared for an emergency. I would always have 1 or 2 tins of soup; 2 tins of meat, 1 of steak for a hot meal, and 1 of corned beef, luncheon meat, or tongue for a cold dish; 1 tin of sardines or other fish; 1 tin of baked beans; 1 tin of spaghetti (ready cooked); 1 or 2 tins or bottles of fruit; 1 tin of peas (garden petits pois are the best); 1 tin of carrots or other vegetable; 1 small tin of potato or Russian salad; 1 tin of evaporated milk; 1 tin of cream.

Store in a cool, dry, and, if possible, dark cupboard. Replace tins as used, but keep stock moving.

FLOUR AND FLOUR PRODUCTS

Biscuits. Keep in an airtight tin away from bread, cakes, and pastry.

Bread. Keep either in bread bin or in a drawer, or wrapped in cloth with plenty of air circulation.

Cakes. Keep in an airtight tin away from other flour products.

Flour. You can choose between *white* and *National flour*. The former gives a lighter texture, the latter is considered by nutritionists to contain more vitamins. It is, however, always recommended that you ask for flour free from agene. *Whole-meal* or *stone-ground flour* (brown flour) is preferred by some people as containing more vitamins. It can be used for all cooking, but it is advisable to add slightly more liquid than when using white flour.

Pastry. Keep in an airtight tin away from other flour products. Never mix cakes with pastry in a tin for the pastry will become very soft.

Herbs to Improve your Cooking

Mention is made in a number of recipes of the more usual herbs, but please regard these recipes as your basic dish, which you can vary according to your particular taste.

Herbs can do more to add additional interest than anything, so if you can cultivate a small herb garden of your own, you will find it very helpful.

Failing this you can buy most of the following herbs dried and sold in tiny drums. Naturally the flavour is not as good, although more concentrated, so use dried herbs very sparingly.

Basil. Rather like bay leaf, and used for same purpose (*see* below).

Bay leaves. These green shiny leaves from the bay tree should be well washed, then put into stews, soups, or even in the milk for a custard. Use about 2 leaves for a stew and 1 for a custard. They can be bought dried, and stored in airtight jars.

Borage. Both the flower and leaf can be used for flavouring fruit or other drinks, and if put into a custard and removed before serving, gives a delicious taste.

Chives. These look like thick blades of grass, have a more delicate flavour than onion, and can be chopped finely and used in omelets and savoury dishes.

Fennel. A very little chopped can be included in a sauce to serve with fish.

Marjoram. These delicate-flavoured leaves are ideal for soups, stuffing, and sauces.

Mint. The perfect accompaniment to lamb (*see* p 113). A little sprig can be put into fruit drinks, and chopped and used in salads.

Parsley. The most useful herb of all to give flavour, and provide a gay garnish.

Rosemary. A sprig put inside a roasting fowl instead of stuffing gives delicate flavour to the flesh.

Sage. Chopped fresh sage leaves are perfect for sage and onion stuffing or giving flavour to savoury dishes.

Thyme. Both ordinary and lemon thyme give a delicious flavour if added to soups or stuffings.

Also remember that you can have a mixture of these herbs, tied in a small piece of muslin and known in cookery as a 'bouquet garni' to give an interesting flavour to most savoury dishes. The 'bouquet garni' is removed before serving.

PRESERVING HERBS FOR THE WINTER

To dry herbs, wash them in hot water after picking, dry well in a cloth, then lay them on baking trays, padded with plenty of paper and a piece of muslin over the top. Dry very slowly in the airing cupboard or very low oven (with the door ajar) until brittle. Crumble and put into jars. In very hot weather they can be covered with muslin and dried in the sun. Parsley is a better colour if dried for a few minutes in a hot oven.

Choosing and Cooking Meat

You will usually find your butcher helpful in showing you the types of meat he has available. The table below explains how to make the best of the different cuts.

BEEF

The lean should be bright red, the fat firm and a pale creamy colour.

Purpose	Cut to Choose	Cooking Time	Accompaniments[1]
Roasting	Sirloin Ribs Fillet Aitchbone (good quality) Topside Rump	15 mins per lb 15 mins over Well-done 20 mins per lb, 20 mins over	Mustard Horseradish sauce Yorkshire pudding

Grilling or
  Frying
	Fillet
	Rump
		10–20 mins,
		depending on
		thickness and
		personal
		preference
			Chipped or mashed
			  potatoes
			Tomatoes

[1] For recipes for accompaniments refer to index under separate items

Stewing or Braising	Skirt or Chuck Bladebone 'Leg of Mutton' cut Brisket Flank	1½ to 3 hours	Mixed vegetables Dumplings Thickened gravy
Pickling or Boiling	Brisket Shin or Leg Silverside Flank Aitchbone	1½ to 3 hours	Vegetables or salad
Stock for Soups	Neck Shin or Leg Clod Marrow bone Oxtail Flank	1½ to 3 hours	

To Carve Beef. Cut thin, large slices across the joint (*see* Pls. 1, 2, 3, for carving Sirloin). The meat should be served with just the thin gravy that comes from the joint when carved, but if a thickened gravy is preferred follow directions on page 42.

MUTTON OR LAMB

The lean is a dull red and firm, the fat white and firm. Lamb is similar but paler in colour.

Purpose	*Cut to Choose*	*Cooking Time*	*Accompaniments*
Roasting	Leg Loin Best end Neck (Lamb) Shoulder Breast, stuffed and rolled	20 mins per lb and 20 mins over	Mutton, redcurrant jelly Lamb, mint jelly Fresh peas
Grilling or Frying	Loin chops Gigot chops[1] Cutlets[1]	10–15 mins	Chipped potatoes Tomatoes Peas
Stewing, Braising or Boiling	Neck Breast Leg Shoulder	1½–2½ hours	Mixed vegetables

[1] Not illustrated on chart, pages 36–37. They come where leg (1) joins loin (2).

Soups, Stocks	Scrag end of Neck Head Trotters	1½–2½ hours

Note. Sheep's head or Lamb's head can also be served (*see* Calf's Head, p 129).

To Carve Mutton or Lamb. Cut large thickish slices downwards. Remove chump bones from saddle before cooking to facilitate carving (*see* Pls. 4, 5, 6). The shoulder is the most difficult joint to cut because of the bone formation (*see* Pls. 7, 8, 9). Hold meat with napkin, which gives better control than a fork. Serve one slice from each part to each person. The meat can be served either with the thin gravy that comes after carving or with a thickened gravy (*see* p 42).

For stuffed loin, see under Pork.

PORK

The lean should be pale pink and the fat white.

Purpose	*Cut to Choose*	*Cooking Time*	*Accompaniments*
Roasting	Loin Leg Bladebone Spare rib	25 mins per lb and 25 mins over	Sage and onion stuffing Apple sauce Orange salad
Frying	Chops from loin Spare rib chops	15–20 mins	Apple sauce Sage and onion stuffing Tomatoes
Boiling	Head Hand and Spring Belly and as for roasting	2½ hours	

Rub joint with salad oil and seasoning before cooking. If stuffing a loin of pork cut rind away thickly, spread stuffing on the meat, replace rind, and tie firmly in several places. Stuffing and meat are then sliced together. Serve with thickened gravy (*see* p 42).

To Carve Pork. For loin, see Pls. 10 and 11. Carve leg and bladebone as for mutton.

VEAL

The lean should be pale pink and dry, the fat firm and white. Cook soon after purchase, for this meat spoils easily.

Purpose	Cut to Choose	Cooking Time	Accompaniments
Roasting	Shoulder Breast Best-end neck Loin Fillet Chump end of loin	25 mins per lb and 25 mins over	Sausages Veal stuffing
Grilling or Frying	Chops from loin Fillet Best end of neck chops	15–20 mins	Chipped potatoes Tomatoes, etc
Stewing or Braising	Breast Fillet Knuckle Middle and scrag end of neck	1½–2½ hours	Mixed vegetables
Boiling	Head Feet Breast	1½–2½ hours	Mixed vegetables
Stock for soups	Feet Knuckle	1½–2½ hours	

To Carve Veal. Cut loin into chops, shoulder downwards as for mutton, and fillet across in thin slices. Serve with thickened gravy (see p 42).

Choosing and Cooking Poultry

When buying poultry see that the flesh is firm and light-coloured. The breast-bone of roasting birds should be soft and pliable. All poultry has thickened gravy (see p 42) if stuffed.

Bird	Cooking Time	Accompaniments
Roasting fowl (chicken)	15 mins per lb and 15 mins over	Veal stuffing Forcemeat stuffing Sausages Bread sauce

Boiling chicken	30–40 mins per lb and 30 mins over (*see* p 105)	White sauce Egg sauce
Duck	15 mins per lb and 15 mins over	Sage and onion stuffing Apple sauce Orange salad
Goose	As duck	As duck
Turkey	For small bird under 12 lb allow 15 mins per lb and 15 mins over For larger birds, 12 mins per lb and 12 mins over	As chicken

To Carve Poultry. Very small ducklings with little flesh should be cut through the centre into two. This is quite easy if you first cut away the wishbone, then cut down on either side of the breastbone. Cut meat on the breast away from the bone and serve each half complete with leg and breast. To carve a family-size duck see Pls. 12, 13, 14. A duck has appreciably less breast than a fowl so cut a thicker slice. If cutting a duck into four portions each gentleman is usually given the leg portion, then the breast bone is cut away and the breast divided into half. To carve turkey see Pls. 15 and 16. For easy carving do not overcook. Carve chicken in the same way as turkey if a large bird. For a small chicken, however, divide each leg into two joints, remove wings, and then cut thicker and fewer slices from sides of breast.

Choosing and Cooking Game

Game should be firm, with clear eyes and smooth fleshy legs. The most useful and usual are Grouse, Pheasant, and Partridge and all of these can be cooked like chicken, except that one does not stuff them, but serves them with bread sauce, game chips (which can be bought in packets and warmed through in the oven), watercress, and fried breadcrumbs.
To fry the breadcrumbs. Heat a little fat in the frying-pan and cook breadcrumbs (*see* p 55) until golden brown.

Allow 15 minutes per lb and 15 mins over to cook the birds. Smaller game birds, pigeons and woodcocks, are roasted for about 25 minutes. Woodcock are served on toast.

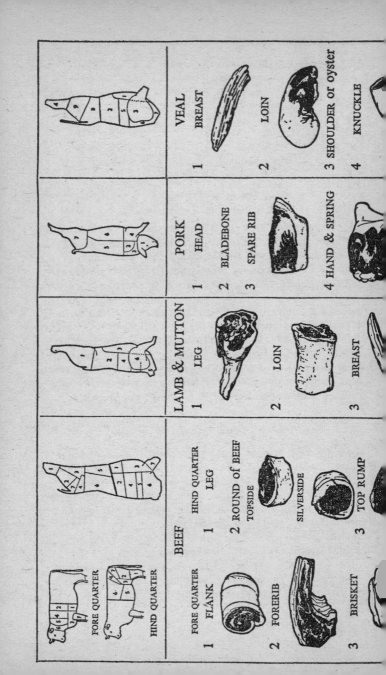

FORE QUARTER

HIND QUARTER

BEEF

HIND QUARTER

1 LEG

2 ROUND of BEEF
TOPSIDE

SILVERSIDE

3 TOP RUMP

FORE QUARTER

1 FLANK

2 FORERIB

3 BRISKET

LAMB & MUTTON

1 LEG

2 LOIN

3 BREAST

PORK

1 HEAD

2 BLADEBONE

3 SPARE RIB

4 HAND & SPRING

VEAL

1 BREAST

2 LOIN

3 SHOULDER or OYSTER

4 KNUCKLE

4 RUMP & FILLET

5 STEAKMEAT

5 FLANK

CHUCK

6 SIRLOIN

WING END OF SIRLOIN

BLADEBONE

7 AITCHBONE

LEG OF MUTTON CUT

6 NECK & CLOD

7 SHIN

of NECK

5 SCRAG END

6 SHOULDER

6 BELLY

7 LEG

6 MIDDLE NECK

7 SCRAG END

8 CHUMP end of LOIN

9 FILLET OF VEAL

THE VARIOUS CUTS
of BEEF, MUTTON, PORK, AND VEAL

Choose your joint according to the type of meal you wish to serve and the amount of time and attention you can give it. *See* 'Choosing and Cooking Meat', pages 31 to 34.

Vegetable	To Choose	To Prepare	To Cook	To Serve
Artichokes, Globe	Crisp and green	Wash well	30 mins in boiling salted water	Melted butter or margarine
Jerusalem	Well-shaped	Peel or scrape	Approx. 20 mins in boiling salted water with juice of lemon to whiten	Melted butter or white or cheese sauce, or use for soup
Asparagus		See p 193	See p 193	See p 193
Beans, Broad	Full pods, firm	When young chop, when older remove pods	20 mins in boiling salted water	Melted butter, parsley sauce
French	Firm crisp pods	When young just cut top and bottom stalks	15 mins in boiling salted water	Melted butter or margarine
Runner	Firm, crisp pods, larger than French beans	Cut into thin slices	Ditto	Ditto
Beetroot	Firm, dark red	Wash	From 1 hour to 2½ hours in boiling salted water. Press to test, don't prick	Hot with white sauce, cold in salads. Can be bought ready cooked
Brussels sprouts	Crisp and firm	Remove outer leaves, wash well, mark with cross at bottom	5–10 mins in boiling salted water	Tossed in margarine

Vegetable	Appearance	Preparation	Cooking	Serving
Cabbage and all cabbage greens, including broccoli	Crisp, green, and firm	Wash and cut into shreds, or sprig	Ditto	Strain, toss in margarine
Cauliflower	White part should be firm and good colour	Wash and divide into flowerets	Ditto	Ditto or with cheese or white sauce
Carrots	Firm, bright orange	Wash and scrape, when older peel. Cut into slices unless very small	In boiling salted water	Brushed with margarine, and chopped parsley in stews, soups
Celeriac	Large, hard	Peel outer skin, cut into dice	In boiling salted water for 15–20 mins	Either raw, or braised with cheese sauce
Celery	Crisp, firm, white	Wash well, remove outer sticks	Ditto	Ditto
Chicory (See Celery)				
Corn on the cob	Leaves – green, corn – bright yellow	Wash well, remove green leaves	10 mins in unsalted water, then add salt	Melted butter
Cucumber	Firm and hard	Peel, cut into slices	Can be boiled for 10 mins	Usually served raw; can be fried – see p 151
Egg plant (Aubergine)	Firm, hard	As Peppers	As Peppers	As Peppers
Endive	Crisp, green (See p 87)	Wash well		Raw in salads
Horseradish		Wash well		

39

Vegetable	To Choose	To Prepare	To Cook	To Serve
Kale (*See* Cabbage)				
Leeks	Firm, white	Wash very well	10–15 mins in boiling salted water	Melted margarine, white or cheese sauce
Mushrooms	(*See* pp 150 and 160)			
Onions	Firm and white[1]			
Parsnips	Firm	Peel, cut into halves or quarters	20–25 mins in boiling salted water, or baked round joint	Melted margarine
Peas	Firm green	Remove pods	10–15 mins in boiling salted water. Add pinch sugar and sprig of mint	Melted margarine
Peppers, Chillies	Tiny, firm, red pods	Wash	Tie in muslin to flavour stew, remove	
Green (unripe)	Firm	(*See* p 133)		
Red (ripe)		(*See* p 133)		
Potatoes: New	Firm, even colour, small; flaking skin	Wash and scrape off skin	Boil for 20 mins *steadily* in salted water with sprig of mint to flavour	Toss well in margarine, garnish with chopped parsley

[1] *See* various recipes in this book.

Potatoes: Old	Good shape and firm	Peel and wash	Boil for 20 mins *steadily* in salted water. Fry, roast, or bake	*See* various recipes
Salsify	Firm and white	Wash and scrape well	30 mins in boiling salted water, with lemon juice	With melted margarine and slices of lemon
Seakale (*See* Celery)				
Spinach	Green and firm	Wash in several lots of water	Boil either in no water except that adhering to leaves or in about ¼ inch. Add little salt	Strain well, mix with little margarine
Swedes	Firm and yellow	Peel, dice	Boil for 25 mins in salted water, strain. Roast for 45 mins— 1 hr round joint	With melted margarine, or cheese sauce, or well mashed
Turnips (*See* Swedes)				
Vegetable Marrow	Smallish, firm	Peel, slice	10 mins in boiling salted water	White or cheese sauce or stuffed (*see* p 151)

Gravy for Meat and Poultry

Having roasted the meat put it onto a very hot dish. Pour away all the fat from the tin except about a tablespoonful. Blend a tablespoonful flour, a good teaspoonful Bisto (or ½ teaspoonful Marmite) with this fat and cook for a few minutes over a low heat – as one does for any sauce. Gradually blend in about ¾ pint stock (little less for thicker gravy) either from cooking the vegetables or from simmering the giblets in the case of poultry. Bring gently to the boil, stirring all the time, and cook until thickened. For a thin gravy for poultry simmer the giblets, then strain the stock.

Choosing and Cooking Vegetables

The golden rule for all vegetable cooking is to use the minimum quantiy of water, have the vegetables in as small pieces as possible, cook in the shortest possible time – with the lid on the pan – and serve as soon as they are cooked (*see* pp 38–41).

Choosing and Cooking Fish

Great care must be taken when shopping for fish to see that it is as fresh as possible. Fish that is freshly caught is fresh in smell, firm, and stiff (not soft and limp), has bright, protruding eyes. Never buy fish if you have any doubts about its freshness. Details of fish in season will be found throughout this book, but as a brief summary here are the groups of fish.

WHITE FISH

Suitable for boiling, savoury dishes (fish pie, etc), grilling, frying, and baking.

Bream. Freshwater fish, rather scarce, but excellent grilled.

Brill. Not unlike turbot. Can be grilled, fried, or baked.

Cod. Excellent all-purpose fish, as it has definite flavour, and cheaper than many.

Flounder. Similar to plaice or sole, and can be used for same purpose, but not such a delicate flavour.

Haddock. Either fresh, when it can be used as cod, or smoked (*see* p 70), a most useful fish with good flavour.

Hake. More delicate flavour, and slightly dearer than cod, but can be used in any way.

Halibut. One of the more expensive fish, though cheaper than turbot, which it rather resembles. Halibut, however, unlike turbot has no spots on the skin. Excellent for grilling, baking.

John Dory. An ugly fish, usually filleted and baked, grilled, or fried.

Plaice. Most useful flat fish, excellent for frying or grilling. Can be recognized by the yellow to reddish-brown spots on the dark skin. Is slightly more rounded in shape than sole.

Rock salmon. An economical fish, nothing like salmon, used as cod.

Skate. An ugly flat fish, generally sold cut into small 'fan' shapes, delicious boiled, fried, or grilled. Before frying steam for a few minutes, then coat with egg and breadcrumbs or batter.

Sole. The most delicate flavoured flat fish, perfect for grilling or frying, or can be steamed between two plates over boiling water, when seasoning should be added.

Turbot. An excellent fish to have cold in a salad, baked, grilled, or fried. Cut into cutlets. It is very substantial, and generally rather expensive.

Whiting. A delicate, fine-flaked fish, very suitable for invalids.

OILY FISH

Herring. With all its other by-products – kippers, herring roes, bloaters – this is an excellent fish, for it is full of food value.

Several ways of cooking herrings are described in this book – they can be baked, grilled, fried, soused, and served cold. A good herring is silver-coloured, very firm, with bright eyes.

Mackerel. Similar to herrings.

Mullet. Red and grey mullet are excellent fish to bake.

Salmon. Cutlets of salmon are delicious served hot, they should be brushed with melted butter and cooked for about 10–15 mins under a hot grill. Serve with new potatoes, green peas, and parsley butter (*see* p 128).

Smelts. A less usual fish today. Can be grilled or fried like herrings.

Sprats. *See* p 103.

Trout. A delicate fish that should be grilled or fried.

Whitebait. Fry as sprats (*see* p 103), but do not remove the heads. Cook until crisp and golden brown. Serve with slices of lemon and brown bread and butter.

SHELLFISH

The greatest care must be taken in choosing shellfish. You will be wise to shop at a fishmonger's where the fish are boiled on the premises. These can be served hot, but for simple dishes serve cold with salads.

Crab. *See* p 145.

Crayfish and Crawfish. As lobster.

Lobster. Get the fishmonger to split the fish and remove the intestinal vein, then remove flesh (as described under Crab, p 145) and dress in the same way.

There is no dark meat with a lobster, but the bright red 'coral' found in a female lobster is delicious.

Oysters. Get the fishmonger to open these for you, serve with paprika or cayenne pepper, slices of lemon, and brown bread and butter.

Prawns. *See* p 126.

Shrimps. As prawns, p 126.

You will find various methods of cooking fish described in this book, and it is not difficult to adapt them to the fish chosen. Remember fish cooks quickly, and is easily overcooked, dried, and spoiled.

Section II

Cookery processes. Terms used in cookery. Weighing and measuring. Quantities to allow. If things go wrong. Foods that have been left over

---

Cookery Processes

You will find all these cookery processes have been used if you work through the recipes in this book, and it is important to understand the principles necessary for each process.

Boiling. When food is boiled, it is put into water, with salt if necessary, and cooked at boiling point, ie, 212 deg F. It is easy to tell when liquid is boiling, for there will be sharp bubbling on the surface.

FISH can be boiled (*see* Fish Pie, p 99) but this is not the ideal way, for flavour is lost. Other methods of cooking are considered better.

MEAT, too, is rarely boiled. We talk about boiled bacon or boiled beef (*see* pp 94 and 110), but in actual fact they are simmered. Stews should also be simmered rather than boiled to ensure that the meat and vegetables are tender. Rapid boiling would result in overcooking on the outside long before the middle of the joint, or pieces of vegetable, were tender.

SOUPS AND SAUCES are generally boiled to thicken, but *simmered* afterwards to prevent the sauce or soup becoming too thick or evaporating.

VEGETABLES should always be cooked *quickly by boiling*, but you will find considerable stress is laid on the *right* way to boil vegetables, ie, in about 1½ inches of water (which must be boiling when the vegetables are put into the pan). The lid should fit tightly, and the vegetables must be cut into small pieces where possible to enable them to cook really quickly, and so retain the maximum amount of vitamin value.

Baking. This term denotes that the food is put into the oven without liquid or fat and cooked in dry heat. Cakes are baked and many of the puddings in this book are baked. You will find instructions for baking potatoes in their jackets on p 88.

FISH. As well as savoury fish dishes, like Fish Pie (p 99), you will find instructions for baking and stuffing fish (p 144). In this case a little moisture and fat are added, but not sufficient to justify altering the name of the method of cooking.

MEAT. We don't bake this, for it is found better to add plenty of fat and *roast*, or liquid and cook in a casserole.

Braising. A form of cooking particularly suitable for meat and some vegetables. (*See* Braised Beef, p 125, and Braised Onions, p 162). The food is first fried in fat, thickening is added, then the cooking continued by gentle stewing.

Frying. At first you may find this form of cookery difficult. People talk about fried foods being greasy, but they will not be if you learn to fry properly.

DEEP FRYING. For deep frying use enough fat to cover the food completely. You will find a description of a deep fat fryer in the list of kitchen utensils on p 13. Although it takes more fat for deep frying it is worthwhile, for the food is cooked more quickly, and therefore tends to be more crisp and dry. Deep frying is ideal for fried fish and chipped potatoes (pp 116, 118).

Always drain food that has been deep fried on crumpled tissue or kitchen paper.

SHALLOW FRYING. This is the form of frying used for bacon, eggs, fish, sauté potatoes (pp 75, 83). Just enough fat to cover the bottom of the pan is used. Make sure the fat is really hot before the food goes into the pan. To test, put in a small piece of bread (about ½ inch square). If this turns a golden brown within a minute, then the fat is hot enough to start cooking. If the bread takes longer than this to brown, then the heat should be increased slightly and the bread tested again. If on the other hand the bread becomes very dark brown quickly, take the frying pan off the heat and allow the fat to cool slightly, then test again.

Serve fried foods quickly, draining off the fat with the help of a fish slice, or in the case of sauté potatoes, drain these on crumpled tissue or kitchen paper. Do not use greaseproof paper, for this will not absorb the fat.

Grilling. Most modern cookers are equipped with a grill, and this is an excellent method of cooking. It uses less fat than frying and is therefore considered less indigestible for many people. It is quick, easy, and clean. Since grilling is a quick operation you will be much more successful with results if you always light the grill several minutes before putting the food underneath. In this way you seal the outside of the food rapidly, and preserve the maximum amount of flavour and moisture inside (*see* Grilled Sole, p 176).

Roasting. This process, like baking, means cooking food in the oven, but roasting means adding fat to keep the meat, poultry, or vegetable moist and sometimes to crisp the outside.

It is not a difficult method of cooking, if you follow the directions for timing and temperature.

Simmering. This process means cooking in water at a slightly lower temperature than boiling – approximately 180 deg. F. Simmering is ideal for large pieces of meat, etc (*see* under Boiling). There is a vast difference between boiling and simmering, and it is very important to remember this for it can make a great deal of difference to the success of your cooking. When the liquid is simmering you will find occasional bubbles on the surface.

Steaming. This means cooking in steam rather than actually allowing the food to come into contact with water. The food tends to be lighter than when it is boiled. A steamer is an excellent piece of kitchen equipment, for you will use it when cooking puddings, etc (*see* Meals in a Steamer, p 185). If you haven't a steamer then put the basin into a pan, with boiling water coming only *halfway* up the container. Put a lid on top, and the conditions are virtually the same as when putting the food into a steamer over boiling water.

Stewing. The food is cooked at simmering point in a small

47

quantity of liquid. For cooking meats, fruit, etc (*see* p 172 for a Beef Stew, and p 122 for stewing fruit).

The advantage is that the flavour of the food is retained; hard fruit or tough meat is made tender and appetizing.

Terms Used in Cookery

It is not necessary for beginners to know all the French and Continental terms that have become associated with more complicated dishes, but several French words are so often used in cookery language that these must be given.

Au gratin. A dish is described as *au gratin* when the top has been covered with crumbs and crisped under the grill or in the oven (example, Cauliflower au Gratin, p 73).

Basting. Some foods, in particular poultry, are inclined to be dry unless fat is poured over at intervals during cooking. This process is known as basting.

Binding. Mixing and holding ingredients together with a thick sauce or egg (*see* Fish Cakes, p 93).

Blanching. Some foods, for example, tripe, have an unattractive appearance unless they are first put into water, brought to the boil, and this water discarded. This initial cooking is called 'blanching'. It is also called 'blanching' when almonds are brought to the boil to remove the brown skins.

Bouquet garni. A small collection of herbs to flavour. *See* under Herbs, p 31.

Clarifying. This means cleaning, and the process is very necessary when using dripping. Cover the dripping with cold water in a rather deep saucepan, bring to the boil, then allow fat and water to cool. You will then be able to lift off the fat, leaving most of the impurities in the water.

As an added precaution it is advisable to turn the piece of clarified dripping upside down on a plate, and scrape away any small particles of food adhering to the bottom with a sharp knife.

Coating. Before frying fish or fish cakes they must be covered, or 'coated', with either a batter (*see* Fried Plaice, p 116) or crisp

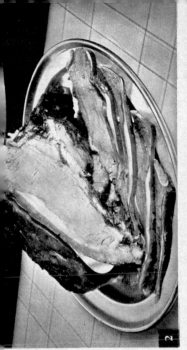

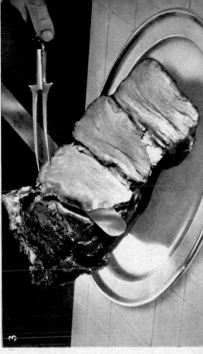

TO CARVE A SIRLOIN OF BEEF

1. Remove the backbone or chine

2. Cut the first slices along the bone

3. Then turn the joint and cut thin or thick slices
   at right angles from the bone. If the joint is boned
   and rolled, cut large, thin slices across the meat
   (Page 32)

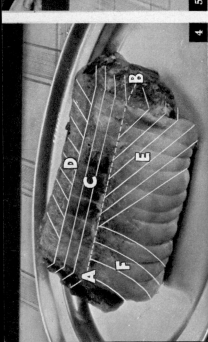

TO CARVE SADDLE OF MUTTON

Cut long slices along lines C. Arrange these on a dish, and then cut from the chump ends A and B. Finally, cut slices in a rather slanting direction, F, E and D. Serve a piece from each part to each person (Page 33)

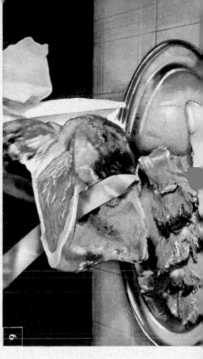

7

8

9

TO CARVE SHOULDER OF MUTTON OR LAMB

7. The dotted lines A, B, F and C show position of bone. To get neat slices carve round this. G indicates meat on blade bone. Cut H in direction of lines

8. Cut at E diagonally

9. Finally, cut D towards forearm part of bone (A) (Page 33)

10

TO CARVE LOIN OF PORK

10. The butcher will almost certainly have sawn through the bones and scored the rind (B). If the rind is not evenly scored, do this with a sharp knife since it aids carving and gives a better 'crackling'.

11. Cut slices downwards (Page 33)

breadcrumbs (*see* Fried Plaice, p 116). To get an even result when the food is fried the coating must be put on quite evenly. A 'coating sauce' is one just sufficiently thick to coat firstly the back of a wooden spoon, then the food. You will find you get this consistency if you use ½ pint liquid to 1 oz flour.

Creaming. In many recipes you will find the instructions 'cream margarine and sugar'. This means beating the ingredients together with a wooden spoon until the margarine is soft and the sugar well dissolved.

Curdling. When a mixture separates it is described as having 'curdled'. Milk 'curdles' when sour. A sauce will curdle if you add acid lemon juice or fruit juice to a very hot or boiling milky base, or egg yolks to a milk or fruit base. Let the mixture cool to just below boiling before stirring fruit, eggs, or anything acid into milky base.

Dripping. This is the fat that runs from meat or bacon during cooking. It is a valuable food and should not be wasted, for you will need it again to add to meat. It must be clarified before storing. To obtain still more dripping melt very fatty pieces of meat down (*see* Rendering down).

Fines herbes. A collection of finely chopped fresh or dried herbs used to flavour foods, omelets in particular.
Description of various herbs on p 30.

Folding. This means a gentle 'flicking' movement. When a recipe states that ingredients should be 'folded' together, it is important to follow this, otherwise you tend to over-beat and spoil the texture.

Grating. Rub foods on a grater until finely shredded. Cheese, for instance, often needs to be grated.

Macedoine. Very small dice of foods; a mixture of diced vegetables is called a macedoine (*see* page 96 for Russian Salad). A mixture or macedoine of mixed fruit makes a delicious fruit cocktail.

49

Mornay. The usual way of describing food served in a cheese sauce.

Panada. This is a very thick sauce, used to bind ingredients together (*see* Durham Cutlets, p 79).

Pinch. In most of the recipes for savoury dishes 'a pinch salt' is given. This means as much salt as can be picked up between the forefinger and thumb. Seasonings must, however, be varied to suit individual tastes.

Poaching. Food cooked in a very small amount of liquid (*see*, for example, Finnan Haddock, p 30).

Puree. A very thick consistency – for example, the fruit purée in Fruit Fool (p 73).

Raspings. The crisp breadcrumbs for coating fish, etc.

Rendering down. As explained under Dripping, when additional fat is required, put fatty pieces of meat in a dish in a low oven and cook *slowly* until all the dripping (or fat) has been obtained, and all that is left is a hard brown piece of gristle. Then clarify (*see* above).

Roux. When making a sauce the fat is first melted, then the flour cooked gently in to explode the starch grains, so ensuring a smooth sauce. The fat and flour mixture is often called 'the roux'.

Sauter. A French word, now commonly used to denote that the food is tossed, and sometimes slightly browned in hot fat (*see* Sauté Potatoes, p 83).

Seasoning. The addition of salt, pepper, and perhaps mustard to food. It is always advisable to err on the side of under-, rather than over-seasoning, for people's tastes vary, and one can always add a little more seasoning at the table.

Shredding. Chopping very finely, and generally in thin fingers. Vegetables, such as cabbage, are shredded to facilitate quick cooking. Nuts are shredded to decorate foods. Use a chopping board and a very sharp knife.

Tossing. This means turning vegetables round in melted margarine or butter so that they are coated with fat. Directions for tossing fish in breadcrumbs to coat are on p 116).

Whisking. Certain ingredients have to be whisked to make them light, for example, an egg white for meringue (*see* Lemon Meringue Pie, p 65). Use an egg whisk, and a vigorous movement.

Weighing and Measuring

Scales or measures are a good investment, for however carefully your mixing and cooking are done, the result may be spoiled if the amounts of ingredients are not accurate. If you have not got scales or measures, however, here are some 'make-do' ways of weighing and measuring:

Cup measures. Use the British Standards Institution cup, if possible. It holds ½ pint. The average teacup holds ¼ pint, or 8 tablespoons.

1 BSI cup or 2 teacups holds:

> ½ pint liquid
> 5–5½ oz flour (loosely packed)
> 8 oz margarine or other fat
> 7½–8 oz sugar
> 8 oz dried fruit
> 16 oz syrup

Spoon measures. Use BSI spoon if possible, or average tablespoon.

> 2 level BSI spoons or tablespoons hold:
>> 1 oz flour, cornflour, cocoa, custard powder
>
> 1¼ level BSI spoons or tablespoons hold:
>> 1 oz sugar
>
> 1 level BSI spoon or tablespoon holds:
>> 1 oz syrup, jam, honey (warm spoon and syrup will drop off easily)

Conversion to the Metric System. The exact conversion of an oz is 28·35 g. but this is a very difficult figure to calculate so it is much more convenient to call 1 oz 30 g. When you come to larger quantities such as 8 oz (½ lb) this is 226·8 g. so that you can call this 225 g. In liquid measures ¼ pint equals 142 ml and it will probably be easier to call this 140 millilitres.

Quantities to Allow

All dishes in this book give average portions for four people. The following guide shows quantities to allow of various goods. Weights given refer to uncooked food.

Fish. Allow 2 fillets each weighing 3–4 oz for each person. For whole fish allow a small sole or plaice about 8–12 oz (which, of course, includes weight of bones) per person. For cutlets of fish allow 6–7 oz per person, and the same amount when buying a large piece of fish for baking.

Meat. For stewing allow approximately 4 oz meat per person (without bone, of course). This is a fairly small allowance, compensated by the vegetables in a stew. Stewing meats are much more economical to buy than other cuts. For grilling, allow a small cutlet in a mixed grill, or a larger one if to be served by itself. When grilling steak allow 4–8 oz, depending on personal appetite, per person. For roasting meat allow about 8 oz meat per person.

Puddings. STEAMED PUDDING. Allow about 1–1½ oz flour per person; for example, a steamed pudding made with 4 oz flour would be enough for 4 people with small appetites or 2 adults and 2 small children. For pastry allow about 1½ oz flour in fruit pies, ie, a pie made with 6 oz flour gives good helpings for 4 people. MILK PUDDINGS. Allow 2–3 oz cereal and 1–1¼ pints milk for four people. For jellies and blancmanges a 1-pint mould should be enough for 4 people.

Soup. If you are having soup, followed by a light snack afterwards, you should allow about ½ pint of cooked soup for each person. If, however, soup is to be the first course of a fairly substantial meal, ¼ pint cooked soup is enough.

Vegetables. POTATOES. The amount of potatoes people eat varies so much that no definite quantity can be advised. As an average allow 2–3 small potatoes per person.

GREEN VEGETABLES. Approximately 4 oz, prepared but uncooked.

ROOT VEGETABLES. Approximately 3 oz, prepared but uncooked.

If Things Go Wrong

I hope you will always find your dishes a perfect success. Don't be too depressed if you have an occasional mishap or failure; remember this happens even to very experienced cooks sometimes, perhaps because the phone rings at the wrong time, or the heat of the cooker was a little greater or less than anticipated.

Sometimes when food appears to have been spoiled it is possible to remedy the fault.

Burned food. This is perhaps the most likely mishap of all. A burned stew or soup, apart from having an unpleasant taste, will have stuck to the bottom of the saucepan. Don't try to scrape the bottom with all the food in the pan, but pour this into a clean saucepan. Taste the soup or stew, and if the burnt flavour is not too pronounced, add a teaspoonful curry powder (dissolved in a little cold water) or Bovril or Marmite. Cook gently again. Put the burnt saucepan to soak with plenty of salt. If a custard or sweet sauce has a burnt flavour you may be able to cover this by adding a few drops almond essence or a little coffee essence.

Lumpy sauce. This is due to undercooking of the flour, or not stirring sufficiently as the sauce came to the boil. Remember it must come *slowly* to the boil, and be stirred all the time. Take your egg whisk, remove the saucepan from the heat, and whisk as hard as you can. This may make it quite smooth, but failing this you must strain the sauce through a fine sieve. Obviously the lumps will contain most of the flour, so the sauce will be very thin. To correct this you must blend a small quantity of flour (about a level dessertspoonful to ½ pint sauce) with 2 tablespoonfuls liquid, add to the sauce, and bring slowly to the boil again, stirring as it thickens.

Note. To keep sauces hot, yet prevent them becoming lumpy or burning, it is advisable to pour the cooked sauce into either the top of a double saucepan or a basin, and keep this hot over a pan of boiling water.

Too much salt. While one always tries to be careful when adding salt to soups, stews, sauces, etc, it does sometimes happen that the amount is too generous. First of all try adding a little milk to the soup or stew (if suitable). This often counteracts the excessive salty taste. If not successful, or if the milk would spoil the recipe, put in several raw potatoes. You will find these absorb the salt as they cook. If the salty taste is very slight in a soup or stew you may find a good pinch of sugar all that is required to balance the flavour.

Undercooked food. MEAT. When temperatures and times for cooking are followed carefully, there will rarely be occasions of either under- or over-cooking, but sizes of meat, quality, etc, do cause slight variations in timing. If you ever find when the meal is quite ready and 'dished-up' that the joint tends to be under-cooked your best plan is to keep vegetables warm in a very low oven, slice the meat thinly, and put this for a few minutes under a hot grill.

POTATOES may sometimes take longer than anticipated. One often finds badly mashed potatoes. If they have been boiled too quickly the outside is very soft and the inside hardly cooked, which makes it impossible to get a smooth, creamy result. If this happens, don't add more water to the half-mashed potatoes – you'll only spoil the flavour. Cover the potatoes with milk. Put over a very low heat, stirring from time to time, and cook for a further 10 minutes. When you are sure the potatoes are all soft, raise the heat to absorb the surplus milk, stir briskly to prevent sticking. This produces the most delicious and creamy mashed potatoes.

Foods that have been Left Over

However carefully one plans the shopping or the meal there are occasions when food will be left. It may be that someone doesn't come in to the meal as expected, and family appetites vary, due to heat, etc. It is generally possible to make good use of the food, and to turn it into appetizing new dishes, for nothing is more monotonous than the same dish re-heated.

Bread. Bread that has become very stale can be used for Apple or other Charlottes (p 142). It can also be sliced and turned into Poor Knight's Fritters – an easy and always delicious pudding (p 191).

If you do not wish to use it for this purpose, make into *breadcrumbs*, put these onto baking trays, and crisp in a very slow oven – Mark 1 or 275 deg. F. When the bread is quite brown and crisp, roll with a rolling pin until fine, then put into jars. These crumbs can be used to coat fish, fish cakes, etc, and will save the expense of buying the ready-prepared raspings. To make breadcrumbs, either crumble with the fingers, or rub the bread up and down against or over a coarse grater, or through a sieve or colander.

Bread and Butter. This can be used for Bread and Butter Pudding (p 119) or served as *French toast* as a change for breakfast. To make this toast brown under a hot grill on the plain side, then put for a minute only with the butter side uppermost. Serve with marmalade or poached eggs.

Eggs. Sometimes a recipe requires only part of an egg, in which case store the yolk carefully by pouring enough cold water to cover over the top. This prevents a skin forming, and the egg yolk keeps for several days. Use in batters for Yorkshire pudding or pancakes (p 86); in scrambled eggs (p. 81); to mix a Kedgeree (p 163); in a steamed pudding mixture (p 52). Egg whites turn a fruit pulp into a delicious sweet (*see* p 162), or can be used for meringue on top of puddings, etc.

Fish. Left-over fish *must* be stored most carefully and used quickly, for it is one of the foods most likely to deteriorate and cause stomach upset. Freshly cooked and good fish can be used for Fish Pie (p 99), for Fish Cakes (p 93), for Fish Soufflé (p 91) or makes delicious Fish Salads (p 135).

Meat. Left-over cooked meat can be used for many and varied dishes. Remember that cold roast meat with good salad is often nicer than the same meat reheated. Store cooked meat carefully (*see* p 28), then use it in one of the many recipes requiring cooked meat in Section III; including Shepherd's Pie (p 89), Curry (p 96), Cornish Pasties (p 126), Durham Cutlets (p 79), Savoury Mincemeat (p 169).

Puddings. JELLIES can be turned into a basin and whisked sharply, adding a little fruit purée, beaten egg white, cream, or the top of the milk. Serve on top of trifle, etc.

MILK PUDDINGS can often be served cold. For example, a rice pudding, if cream or the top of the milk is beaten well into it, can be divided between individual glasses, topped with fruit, and makes a delicious sundae. For a second hot milk pudding, add the yolk of an egg to about $\frac{1}{2}$ pint cold left-over milk pudding, then *fold* in the stiffly beaten egg white. Bake in a dish in the centre of a moderate to moderately hot oven, Mark 5–6 or 375–400 deg. F., for 25 minutes and you will have a delicious Soufflé Pudding.

SPONGE OR SUET PUDDINGS. Cut the remainder of the pudding into neat slices. Dip in a little beaten egg, then crisp breadcrumbs. Fry until golden brown and serve with golden syrup or hot jam, or fruit.

Sandwiches. Wrap sandwiches in moist lettuce leaves, then in greaseproof paper. If you have a refrigerator put them into a covered container, failing this into an airtight tin. You will find them perfect the next day. Left-over sandwiches can also be toasted or fried. Put on the grill, toast the sandwich on either side, and serve at once. To fry, heat a little margarine in the frying-pan, fry on both sides until golden brown, then serve at once.

Soup. Soup deteriorates very quickly, so always store most carefully (*see* p 72). If serving again the next day, remember to add a little different flavouring, for example, one or two tomatoes in a vegetable soup, a little Marmite in a meat soup, so that it is slightly different from the preceding day. Many soups, if not too thick, are excellent served cold on a hot day. If you have a refrigerator the soup can be poured into the freezing tray and left until partly iced.

Vegetables. GREEN VEGETABLES. From a health point of view do not re-heat green vegetables if you can avoid it. If some are left they can be used with potatoes for 'Bubble and Squeak' (p 109). POTATOES can always be re-heated in a different form – Potato Cakes (p 104), Sauté Potatoes (p 83). While cold potatoes are not so good for a potato salad, they can be used for this (p 67). ROOT VEGETABLES can be served cold in salads. Swedes, carrots, can be mashed and used instead of mashed potatoes in Shepherd's Pie (p 89).

Section III

Seasonal foods and menus. Christmas catering. Using special parts of your cooker. Dinner parties. Buffet parties. Picnics

---

I hope newcomers to the kitchen and cookery will enjoy working through this section of the book.

It has always seemed to me a mistake to divide foods into water-tight sections, ie, soups, fish dishes, meat dishes, vegetable cookery, etc, when writing for beginners, for it gives very little help in 'coordinating' the various ingredients that go to make up a complete meal. That is why I felt it would be much more helpful if I gave a few representative menus for each month of the year, so giving a chance to 'spotlight' the foods that should be at their best and cheapest at that particular period. The fact that I suggest roast pork as a main dish in January doesn't mean it won't be served at other times throughout the year, but you will then be able to substitute appropriate vegetables for those suggested in January.

January Shopping

At this time of the year, when the weather is generally cold, and one's resistance low after the winter months, it is essential to plan nourishing and sustaining meals. Stews, casserole dishes, home-made soups are all suitable, but remember to serve plenty of freshly-cooked vegetables and fruit to build up the family so that they are equipped to fight flu and colds.

FOODS IN SEASON

Eggs are beginning to get more plentiful after the late autumn shortages, so make good use of these.

Fish. Most fish is fairly expensive owing to high seas. The best varieties to buy are: WHITE FISH. Cod, haddock, hake, halibut, skate, sole, turbot. OILY FISH. Herrings, sprats, whitebait. SHELLFISH. Crayfish, oysters, scallops, shrimps.

Fruit. Apples, lemons, oranges all plentiful. Imported pears and the first of the forced rhubarb will be available.

Meat. Most meat available. Pork is generally good at this time of the year. Rabbits are in season only until end of the month, except imported ones.

Vegetables. GREEN. Brussels sprouts, cabbage (cabbage greens of all kinds), cauliflower, kale, mushrooms. Spinach will be available if the weather is reasonably good. ROOT VEGETABLES. Artichokes (Jerusalem), carrots, celeriac, celery, chicory, onions, parsnips, swedes, turnips.

January Meals

JANUARY FIRST

This being the beginning of the menu section you will find full instructions for those items on the menu required day after day, eg, tea, coffee, toast. Because they are so usual it is often felt they are dull and unimportant, but please don't get into the habit of thinking like this. Good coffee, a good pot of tea, really crisp toast should be prepared as carefully as an elaborate meal.

Breakfast
Porridge   Boiled Eggs
Toast   Marmalade
Tea or Coffee

Breakfast Hints

Unless your family have porridge every morning it is wise when you are new to cooking to have this only when the main dish needs no attention at all. You will soon be able to look after several things at once, but until you feel competent and confident to do this it is wiser to make everything as straightforward as possible. Your first job when you come down is to get the water heating for tea or coffee. Then put on the grill, so that it will be thoroughly hot before you make the toast, for slow cooking of bread gives a hard, leathery result.

Porridge
For four people

You can use the excellent 'Quick Quaker' oats, which cook in just over a minute. Follow the directions on the packet. You can, however, use rolled oats, which take a little longer.

ROLLED OATS

3 teacups rolled oats. 2 teacups cold water. 4 teacups or 1 pint boiling water. Good pinch salt.

Put the rolled oats into the saucepan then, using a wooden spoon, gradually stir in the cold water, until you have a smooth paste. Add the boiling water carefully, again stirring to prevent the porridge becoming lumpy. Put the saucepan on the heat, adding the salt, and cook steadily for about 6–8 minutes. This means you must not have too great a heat and must stir from time to time.

Many people prefer to use oatmeal for their porridge.

OATMEAL PORRIDGE

2 tablespoonfuls medium or coarse oatmeal. ½ teacup cold water. 1 pint boiling water. Good pinch salt.

Blend the oatmeal with the cold water in the saucepan, stirring well. Gradually add the boiling water and the salt. Put over a fairly high heat, and stir until the mixture comes to the boil. Continue stirring for about five minutes until the porridge has thickened well, then put a lid on the saucepan, lower the heat, and cook gently for ½ hour. Obviously if you prefer this type of porridge you must get it cooking before attending to anything else for breakfast, or partly cook it the night before, then just warm it through gently the next day.

Double Saucepan for porridge. To save stirring the porridge you may like to make it in a double saucepan (*see* description of this on p 15). Mix the porridge in the upper container, fill the bottom pan with boiling water, or allow water to come to the boil. Allow about twice the usual cooking time.

Boiled Eggs

Most people like their eggs just set, in which case they will take
3½ minutes. Allow 4 minutes if you know the eggs are very fresh.
An egg required to be rather under-set and liquid should have
about 3 minutes. A very firm egg, ie, hard-boiled, needs about
7 minutes. Put enough water into a small saucepan to cover the
eggs. Bring this to the boil, then gently lower the eggs into the
boiling water. Time carefully and serve at once. If you find one
of the egg shells cracking, immediately put about a tablespoonful
of vinegar into the water; this prevents the egg coming out of
the shell and spoiling. You can adjust the cooking time according
to personal taste.

To Make Good Toast

Before cutting the bread make sure the grill is hot. Put the bread
on the grid in the grill pan and hold it under the grill until brown.
Turn over and do the same the other side. If you have an electric
toaster, follow directions for particular make. When the toast is
cooked don't lay it flat on plates or the kitchen table, for the hot
toast causes moisture to form and makes it limp and soggy. Give
the toast a good bang on each side to let the steam out, then stand
it up at once in a toast rack. If you have no rack, then support
it against the back of the cooker until cold. Try not to make the
toast too soon before breakfast, for it spoils with long waiting.

To Make Tea

1. Draw fresh cold water into the kettle, don't use the hot tap.
2. When the water is getting hot in the kettle, pour a little into
   the teapot to warm it thoroughly.
3. Pour out the water, and allow 1 teaspoonful tea to each person
   and if a fairly strong brew is liked 1 extra teaspoonful. This
   should be done as the kettle starts to boil.
4. Watch the kettle carefully, and *the moment* the water is boiling
   pour it over the tea.
5. Put on the lid of the teapot and let the tea infuse (ie, stand)
   in a warm place for about 5 minutes.

Some people like to strain the tea after 5 minutes into a second
hot pot, so that there is no danger of it tasting over-infused (or

over-brewed). This makes extra work and is not necessary if timing is correct. It is wise economy to buy the best brand of tea you can afford. You may have to try one or two makes before you find *the* tea that suits your family. While most people like Indian tea for breakfast some like a China tea at teatime. This gives a weaker brew, and has a less 'biting' taste. Serve Indian or China tea with cold milk if wished, but if you like China tea you may prefer it with no milk and slices of lemon.

To Make Good Coffee

At one time it was considered almost impossible to get a good cup of coffee in a British household. That, of course, was an exaggeration, for many people can and do make excellent coffee. There is no reason why coffee should not be good in this country for we have good blends. The whole fault was that people were not prepared to take the time and trouble. There are a number of ways of making good coffee, but these are the essentials:

1. Use the right amount of coffee – 4 heaped dessertspoonfuls to 1 pint water.
2. Use freshly-drawn water for coffee as you do for tea.
3. Bring the water just to the boil, but don't let it boil for any length of time.
4. When the water has been added to the coffee it should *never* be allowed to boil together. This gives a bitter taste.
5. Buy your coffee in small quantities, for it deteriorates with keeping. Transfer it from opened packets to screw-topped jars.
6. Try not to make more coffee at one time than you will use.
7. Serve coffee with hot or cold *but never boiling* milk.

Method No 1 – with a jug

First pour a little hot water into the jug to warm it. After a minute or so pour this away, put in the coffee. Pour over the right quantity of freshly boiling water, put the lid on the jug or cover with a clean cloth. After 1 minute stir the coffee and leave to infuse for about 5 minutes in a warm place. The coffee grounds sink to the bottom of the jug, but to make sure your coffee is extra clear you can either strain into a second jug or strain into the cups. You can use a Melio coffee jug or pot for this method. It has an automatic filter that strains the coffee and makes sure no grounds come into your cup.

METHOD NO 2 – WITH A SAUCEPAN

Put the coffee into a saucepan, pour on the cold water. Bring steadily to boiling point, but do not actually boil. Take the saucepan off the heat, but keep in a warm place for a minute. Stir well, then cover and allow to infuse for about 5 minutes. Strain into a warmed pot or into the cups.

Main Meal of the Day (Lunch or Dinner)

Roast Pork[1]
Apple Sauce   Sage and Onion Stuffing
Boiled Potatoes[2]   *Brussels Sprouts*[3]
Lemon Meringue Pie

PLAN OF WORK

1. Make pastry case; this could be done the day before, if wished.
2. Prepare onions for stuffing.
3. Prepare apples for sauce, and vegetables.
4. Put meat into oven, which would be pre-heated.
5. After about ¾ hour put stuffing into oven. Put plates, etc, to warm.
6. Prepare filling for Lemon Meringue Pie, put into oven (unless made day beforehand).
7. Put on water for potatoes.
8. Put in potatoes.
9. Put on apples, etc, for sauce.
10. Put on water for sprouts.
11. Put in sprouts. Whip egg whites.
12. Dish up meat, and stuffing, make gravy, put dishes to soak.
13. Dish up vegetables, and sauce, put saucepans to soak.
14. Put ready-mixed meringue over lemon pie and put into oven.
15. Take first course to the table.

Note. As you see, I have assumed you are making and baking the

[1] *See* Meat table, p 33.   [2] and [3] *see* Vegetable table, pp 41 and 38.

Lemon Meringue Pie the same day, but this could be made beforehand.

Roast Pork

Put the meat into the roasting tin, making sure the butcher has 'scored' the fat, to give good crackling. Rub this with a little margarine paper, which ensures that the crackling will be brown and crisp. Set the oven for hot, Mark 6–7 or 425–450 deg. F.,[1] and keep at this temperature for the first 30 minutes of cooking time. After this the heat can be reduced slightly to Mark 5 or 375–400 deg. F. (moderately hot). Put the meat in the hottest part of the oven (*see* diagrams, p 19).

Apple Sauce

¾ lb apples. ½ oz margarine. Tablespoonful sugar. Water.

You may find it worthwhile to prepare a few extra apples for the Apple Fool for the second day's menu (if you should be following this book exactly). Peel the apples thinly, cut into quarters, removing the cores. Slice thinly, then put into a small saucepan, adding about a teacup water, the margarine, and the sugar.

When ready to cook (ie, about 15–20 minutes before the meal is ready) allow to simmer steadily until a smooth mixture. If more convenient this can be cooked in a double saucepan, so eliminating any risk of scorching the bottom of the pan. Beat well with wooden spoon when the apples are cooked to give good appearance.

Sage and Onion Stuffing

2 large onions (peeled). 1 teacup breadcrumbs.[2] 1 oz suet. 1 teaspoonful dried sage. 1 egg. Good pinch salt and pepper.

Put the onions into a saucepan, adding about ½ pint water. Simmer steadily for about 20 minutes, when the onions will be partly cooked. Remove from the water onto chopping board and chop up into small pieces. Transfer to a basin, then add all the other ingredients. I expect you will be using the shredded suet, but if it is in a piece chop this also. You can either put this on the piece of pork after it has been roasting for about ¾ hour or put into a

[1] Individual ovens vary, so all heats given are approximate.
[2] *See* p 55.

separate dish. The stuffing will then be ready to dish up at the same time as the meat.

Lemon Meringue Pie

FOR THE PASTRY: *6 oz flour (preferably plain). 1½ oz lard. 1½ oz margarine. Good pinch salt. Water to mix.* FOR THE FILLING: *2 lemons. 2 level tablespoonfuls cornflour or custard powder. Cold water. 2 eggs. 3 tablespoonfuls sugar. 1 oz margarine.*

HOW TO MAKE GOOD SHORT-CRUST PASTRY

1. Sieve the flour into a mixing bowl, together with the salt.
2. Cut the margarine and lard into about 5 pieces, then drop these into the flour.
3. Rub with the tips of your fingers only, until the mixture looks like fine breadcrumbs. *Don't over-handle.*
4. Gradually stir in a little cold water with a knife. You will use somewhere about 1½ tablespoonfuls cold water, but this varies a lot according to flour, etc, so add about ½ tablespoonful, mix, then feel with the tips of your fingers. When the mixture rolls into a ball and leaves the mixing bowl clean it is ready. Too dry pastry is difficult to roll out, for it cracks. Too wet pastry sticks to the pastry board and rolling pin, and you need to sprinkle a lot of flour on it. This may make it heavy.
5. Lightly dust the rolling pin and pastry board with flour from your flour dredger.
6. Put on the pastry, roll out to desired shape.

For the Lemon Meringue Pie roll out the pastry to line a flan ring (*see* Pl. 23) or a deep sandwich tin. When the pastry is fitted into the tin, put on a piece of greased paper – greasy side touching the pastry – and lay on this some haricot beans or about three or four crusts of bread (*see* Pls. 17, 18); this keeps the bottom of the pastry flat. Bake in the centre of a hot oven – Mark 6–7 or 425–450 deg. F. – for about 15 minutes. Remove from the oven and carefully take out the paper and crusts, then return to the oven for a further 5–10 minutes, until pale golden colour. If you use an ovenproof dish, it is advisable to stand this dish on a flat baking sheet to help in browning the bottom of the pastry. Before putting in the lemon filling remove the flan ring, or lift out of the sandwich tin by carefully turning upside down.

Rub the lemons against the sides of a fine grater to remove all the yellow rind (known as the 'zest'). Cut the lemons into halves, and press each half onto a lemon squeezer until you have extracted all the juice. Pour the juice into a measure, add the lemon rind, then put in enough water to give you ½ pint liquid all together. Measure the custard powder or cornflour into a basin, gradually stir in the liquid. Put into a saucepan and cook gently over a steady heat, stirring all the time to keep the mixture smooth. It is ready when thick and clear. Let it *cool slightly*, then gradually stir in the egg yolks.

To separate the egg whites from the yolks. Break the eggshell carefully in the centre – it must be done gently to make certain you don't break the yolk. Hold the egg over a basin, and slowly tip the yolk from one half of the shell to the other. Do this several times until you are sure all the egg white has dropped into the basin. As the egg whites are going to be whipped the basin must be perfectly dry, for moisture or a small quantity of yolk will prevent the whites whipping properly. When the yolks have been stirred into the lemon mixture this filling should be spread over the pastry and the flan returned to a moderate oven, Mark 4–5 or 350–375 deg. F., for about 10 minutes. When ready to make the meringue, whisk the egg white for about 5 minutes until very stiff, so stiff that the mixture stands up in peaks in the basin. It helps if you use a large basin or mixing bowl. Fold in nearly all the sugar. If you have to whip the egg whites some little time before baking – as you may have to if following the Plan on p 63 – don't add the sugar until the last minute, and give a quick last-minute whisk before doing this. Pile the meringue over the lemon filling, keeping it against the pastry. Dust the last of the sugar over the top, then put the sweet into the oven.

If you wish to set the meringue while having the first course of your meal, turn an electric oven *Off* – opening the oven door, to lose some of the heat, for a few minutes. With a gas oven reduce the heat by opening the door for a few minutes, then re-set thermostat to Mark 2 or 3. The meringue should be a golden colour when ready to serve.

As this is a fairly ambitious sweet you may prefer to cook it separately and eat it hot or cold.

Meringues, if they are to be served cold, must be set slowly, so that they are crisp right through. This would be the timing: Hot oven – Mark 6–7 or 425–450 deg. F. – for 15 minutes for pastry, then remove paper, etc, and return to oven for 5 minutes. Moderate oven – Mark 4–5 or 350–375 deg. F. – for 10 minutes for the filling. Open oven door to reduce heat. Very cool oven – Mark 1 or 275 deg. F. – for about 40 minutes to set meringue. The sweet could be re-heated gently on the next day.

Light Lunch or Supper
Cold Meat
Potato Salad   Green Salad

Even in winter salads are appreciated, and if the day should be a Sunday a simple evening meal will probably be preferred. Sliced cheese could be substituted for meat.

Slice the meat thinly and arrange on the plates garnished with a slice of tomato or lettuce leaf.

Potato Salad

There is an old saying, 'Make a potato salad hot and eat when cold', which is perfectly true. Many people use cold potatoes for their salad, but they do not absorb the flavour of the mayonnaise or salad dressing as well, so it is worthwhile making the salad while the potatoes are hot. You can cook extra potatoes for the main meal, and have onion and mayonnaise ready to add the necessary amount to the diced potatoes.

For four people allow about 6 medium-sized boiled potatoes (*see* p 40). Drain well, and while hot cut into neat squares. They may crumble a little but if you have cooked them steadily (remember, a potato rapidly boiled is a potato spoiled) they should keep a reasonable shape. Put into a bowl, add about 1 teacup mayonnaise or salad dressing (*see* p 69), then about 2 teaspoonfuls finely grated onion (rub the peeled onion against your coarse grater, if very fine holes are used it becomes a pulp). Add good pinch salt and pepper. Stir in about a tablespoonful chopped parsley. In winter months parsley may be difficult to obtain so use about ½ teaspoonful dried mint and ½ teaspoonful dried parsley. Put into salad dish. Just before serving dust the top with chopped parsley or paprika pepper.

To chop parsley use a rather large chopping knife, holding it with your fingers on top of the tip. Keep your left hand holding this fairly steady, but move your right hand, which will be holding the handle, backwards and forwards until parsley is chopped. Modern dietitians recommend using kitchen scissors, since in this way you lose none of the juice, from which valuable vitamin is obtained.

Green Salad

Use well-washed lettuce, watercress, or mustard and cress, tomatoes, and sliced apple (dessert apple, if possible). At this time of the year cucumbers are very costly, so to give additional colour you could put in quarters of orange. To prepare the lettuce remove bottom of stalk with a knife, then pull leaves apart with your fingers.

To prepare watercress just cut off bottom of stalks and discard any yellow leaves; if fresh all leaves will be green. To prepare mustard and cress cut off bottom of stalks. Put the salad greens into separate lots of cold water, adding a pinch of salt. Soak for about 15 minutes.

Put lettuce and watercress in a salad shaker and twirl this round out of doors until surplus moisture has been absorbed, or, failing a salad shaker, use a clean tea cloth. Mustard and cress should be put into a fine sieve and put under running cold water to get rid of little brown seeds. Dry in cloth.

Arrange the salad on a flat dish or in a salad bowl, making an attractive pattern. Don't do this until a fairly short time before the meal, for it is far better to keep the salad ingredients in a cool place. You can also add one or two sliced hard-boiled eggs. Instructions for boiling eggs are on p 61, but after cooking the eggs for 7–8 minutes take them out of the saucepan and plunge into cold water. This rapid cooling prevents a dark rim forming round the yolk of the egg. Crack the eggshells when cool enough to handle, but don't peel or slice until cold, otherwise the eggs may break. You can buy egg slicers, but failing these use a sharp knife.

Salad Dressings

At first you may not wish to make your own salad dressing or mayonnaise, and there are good products to be bought. Try several varieties until you find the one you will prefer. If you feel you can spare time to make your own here is a cooked salad dressing that keeps well in a cool place.

1 oz flour. 2 oz butter or margarine. 1 or 2 eggs. 1 tablespoonful lemon juice or vinegar. ½–1 teaspoonful sugar. ½ teaspoonful salt. Good pinch pepper and dry mustard. Just under ½ pint milk.

Heat the margarine or butter in a saucepan. Take the pan off the heat and carefully stir in the flour. Cook the roux for a few minutes over a steady heat, then once again take the pan off the heat, and gradually add the cold milk. Return to the heat and stir well as the sauce comes to the boil. Cook until thickened, then stir in the seasoning and sugar. When the sauce has cooled slightly add the beaten egg or eggs and lemon juice or vinegar. Pour into bottle and store in a cool place.

MAYONNAISE

Yolk of an egg. Good pinch salt, pepper, and mustard. 4–8 tablespoonfuls olive oil. 1 dessertspoonful vinegar. 1 dessertspoonful warm water.

Put the egg yolk and seasonings into a basin. Gradually beat in the oil, drop by drop, stirring all the time until the mixture is thick. When you find it creamy stop adding oil, for too much will make the mixture curdle. Beat in the vinegar gradually, then the warm water. Use when fresh.

FRENCH DRESSING

This dressing is delicious over lettuce and a green salad, instead of the heavier salad dressing or mayonnaise. Adapt the amount of oil and vinegar, if you wish, to suit your own taste.

1 dessertspoonful olive oil. 1 dessertspoonful vinegar. Good pinch salt, sugar, dry mustard, and pepper.

Mix the seasonings, including the sugar, with the oil, then work in the vinegar.

JANUARY SECOND

Breakfast

Grapefruit
Smoked Finnan Haddock
Toast[1]   *Marmalade*[2]
Tea or Coffee[3]

To prepare grapefruit

Cut the grapefruit in halves, allowing half per person. Use either a small pair of scissors or sharp vegetable or fruit knife, and slit between the sections of fruit, so making them easy to remove with the spoon. Take out the centre pith and 'core'. If you are sure everyone likes sugar sprinkle a little over the fruit and let it stand for as long as possible; this gives it a better flavour. Serve extra sugar if wished. To make the grapefruit look more attractive put half a glacé cherry or a whole fresh cherry, when in season, in the centre. Stand in grapefruit glasses.

Preparation of grapefruit takes quite a time, so you may like to do it overnight, covering the fruit with a cloth or putting into the refrigerator so that it is well chilled.

Smoked Finnan Haddock

Cut off the side fins and tail of the fish, then divide into the required number of portions. Put water into a saucepan and when boiling put in the fish. Cook steadily for about 5 minutes. Strain well with a fish slice and put on to hot plates. Put a good knob of margarine on top before serving. Don't salt the water since smoked fish has a 'salty' flavour. If preferred the pieces of fish could be put into a baking dish and half covered with milk. Put a margarined paper on top of the dish and bake in a moderate to moderately hot oven, Mark 5–6 or 375–400 deg. F., for about 10–12 minutes.

Main Meal of the Day (Lunch or Dinner)

Steak and Kidney Pudding
Creamed Potatoes (also called Mashed Potatoes)   Cabbage[4]
Apple Fool

[1] *See* p 61.   [2] *See* p 205.   [3] *See* p 61.
[4] *See* Vegetable table, p 39.

1. Make the suet crust just after breakfast. Put on water to boil.
2. Line basin, put in filling, as instructed in recipe.
3. Put basin into steamer over boiling water.
4. At convenient time prepare Apple Fool. Watch pudding and fill up pan with boiling water during cooking.
5. Just over half an hour before meal put on water for potatoes.
6. While water is coming to boil prepare vegetables.
7. Put in potatoes.
8. Put on water for cabbage.
9. Put in cabbage.
10. Dish up potatoes and cream them (p 72).
11. Dish up cabbage and save stock (*see* instructions under Steak and Kidney Pudding, p 72).
12. Dish up pudding.

Steak and Kidney Pudding

FOR THE SUET PASTRY: *8 oz flour (with plain flour use 1 teaspoonful baking powder). 4 oz shredded suet. Good pinch salt. Water to mix.*

FOR THE FILLING: *¾–1 lb stewing steak. 2 lamb's kidneys or 3–4 oz ox kidney. Seasoning. Water or stock.*

Put the flour and pinch of salt through a sieve into a basin. Add the shredded suet and mix with your fingers. If you are using butcher's suet, this should be chopped finely (on a floured board with a knife dipped in flour so that it does not stick) or rubbed against a coarse grater. Stir the suet well into the flour, then gradually stir in enough cold water to make a firm dough. Put in the water slowly, for if too sticky the pastry cannot be rolled out.

Then roll out the pastry on a floured board with a lightly floured rolling pin, until it is less than ¼ inch thick. Lower the piece of pastry into a 1¼–1½ pint basin and press it against the sides, try to keep it flat without folds, otherwise the pudding crust will be too thick (*see* Pl. 20). Cut off the surplus, for you will need that for the lid. Cut the steak into thin pieces, and the kidney into small dice. Put about a level tablespoonful flour and the good pinch salt onto a plate and mix them together. Put a layer of meat in the pudding, then a sprinkling of the seasoned

71

flour. Fill the basin like this until all meat is used. Cover with enough water or stock (*see* below) nearly to fill the basin. Re-roll the last of the pastry, and make into a round large enough to cover the top of the basin. Put this over the pudding, press the edges of the lid to the edges of the side pastry. Cover with a piece of greased paper, greasy side against the pudding. Put into a steamer over a pan of boiling water, and cook for about 3½–4 hours. For the first 1½ hours the water must boil rapidly under the pudding, after that it can boil more steadily for the rest of the cooking time. Watch the saucepan, and fill up with boiling water as it gets low. If you have no steamer stand the pudding in a saucepan with the water coming halfway up the basin. Fill up frequently.

When ready to dish up the pudding, lift carefully from the steamer onto the kitchen table. Dry the basin then lift onto a hot plate, and to give the finishing touch arrange a folded serviette round the basin. Never turn out the pudding. Heat a little more stock or the water from cooking the cabbage and serve in a sauce boat. When the first slice of pudding is cut out, pour in the stock to give more gravy.

To make stock. In this and many other recipes in the book mention is made of stock. This is liquid used as a basis for good soups and gravies and meat dishes. When short of this mix a small quantity of Marmite or Bovril with hot water to provide flavour.

To get a real bone stock put a large marrow bone or several meat bones (which you can obtain from the butcher) into a large pan. Cover with water, add salt and pepper to taste, and simmer steadily for about 2 hours. You can add one or two onions and carrots to give flavour, but the additional vegetables are inclined to make the stock go bad more quickly. Strain the stock when ready *and keep in a cold place*. If you have no refrigerator it should only be kept for a day or so and brought to the boil each day if the weather is hot. Soup is stored in the same way.

Creamed (or Mashed) Potatoes

Approximately 1–1¼ lb potatoes. ½–1 teacup milk. 1–2 oz margarine. Salt.

Boil the potatoes as instructed in the vegetable table on p 40. Strain off the water. Using a fork, beat the potatoes until quite soft and smooth. The best mashed potatoes are made if you heat the milk, but whether hot or cold, beat in the milk slowly until the potatoes begin to turn a snowy white and fluffy. A wooden spoon is best for this, and funnily enough a draught from an open door or window helps to turn the potatoes white. When you are satisfied they are quite smooth beat in the margarine. Although you will have cooked the potatoes in salted water you may find you need an additional pinch salt and pepper to give flavour. Pile the potatoes into a hot dish, forking them into a neat pattern. Dust the top with paprika pepper or chopped parsley.

Apple Fool

½ pint sweetened thick apple pulp. ½ pint thick sweetened custard, made as directions with custard powder. Good squeeze of lemon juice. A few glacé cherries and tiny pieces of angelica.

If you have thick apple sauce left from the menu for January First you could make use of this. You will find you can often save yourself trouble if you cook a little extra fruit, etc, to make fruit fools later. To make the apple pulp specially, peel, core, and slice just under 1 lb cooking apples. Put them into a saucepan with only about ½ teacup water and sugar or golden syrup to taste. Most people will like a good tablespoonful of sweetening. Cook gently so that they will not burn. When the apples are smooth, beat well with a wooden spoon, adding the lemon juice. When the custard is cold (this should be sweetened too) and the apple is cold beat them together with a wooden spoon. Put into four glasses and decorate on top with cherry and angelica. This light sweet is ideal after the rather solid Steak and Kidney Pudding.

Light Lunch or Supper
Cauliflower Au Gratin

For a main dish you will need 1 large cauliflower or 2 small ones. FOR THE CHEESE SAUCE: 1 oz margarine. 1 oz flour. ½ pint milk or ¼ pint milk and ¼ pint veg. stock. 2–3 oz grated cheese. Good pinch salt, pepper, and mustard. 1 tablespoonful crisp breadcrumbs.

Cook the cauliflower according to directions in vegetable table on p 39, leaving the sprigs fairly large as the dish looks more interesting this way. Drain it well, and if you prefer you may use the vegetable stock, which will be about $\frac{1}{4}$ pint, instead of all milk. To retain the most vitamins for this dish it is advisable to start the sauce while the cauliflower is cooking. Start off by making a *white sauce*, which is the foundation for cheese and many other sauces. Heat margarine in a saucepan over a low heat, and when melted take off the heat and stir in the flour. Make sure all the flour is absorbed by the margarine, otherwise there is a danger of the roux burning or discolouring. Return to the heat and cook gently for 3 minutes, stirring all the time. Once again take the pan off the heat and gradually stir in either the $\frac{1}{2}$ pint *cold* milk or, if adding cauliflower stock, the $\frac{1}{4}$ pint cold milk Bring the mixture slowly to the boil, stirring all the time. When the sauce has boiled for several minutes it will thicken enough to form a coating over the back of a spoon; this is called a coating consistency. Add seasoning and most of the cheese. If you are using cauliflower stock bring the sauce just to the boil, strain the cauliflower quickly, stir in the hot stock, and seasoning, then most of the cheese.

Note. If at any stage your sauce seems to be lumpy give it a sharp whisk. But if you cook the flour as directed, add the milk slowly, and stir all the time the sauce is cooking, it will keep smooth.

Arrange the hot cauliflower in a hot dish, pour over the cheese sauce, making sure it soaks through into the vegetable. Sprinkle the last of the cheese and the breadcrumbs on top and put under a hot grill for a few minutes to brown the top. Serve at once. If you have been a little slow about making the sauce, etc, and the cauliflower has become slightly cold, you must heat the dish and brown it for 15 minutes near the top of a moderate to moderately hot oven, Mark 5–6 or 375–400 deg. F., but in doing this you tend to over-cook the cauliflower. Serve with crisp toast or, if you like, with another vegetable.

JANUARY THIRD

Breakfast

Ready-cooked Cereal
Fried or Grilled Bacon and Egg
Toast, etc

Having put on water for tea or coffee, make the toast, for frying bacon and egg takes only a short time, and they are spoiled if kept hot for long. Make sure plates are put to warm either in the plate rack or under grill.

To FRY BACON AND EGGS. When cooking rashers of bacon cut off the rinds. You will find this easy to do if you use a pair of scissors. Lay the rashers of bacon in your frying-pan – with the rinds – for they will produce fat for frying the eggs. You will cook the bacon better and keep it more moist if you lay the lean part of the second rasher over the fat part of the first. Fill the pan like this. Fry quickly until the bacon just begins to curl at the edges. Lift onto hot plates, and while you are doing this leave in the rinds to cook out all the fat. You should have sufficient fat to coat the bottom of the pan; if, however, you feel there is not enough add a small quantity of dripping or lard (about the size of an acorn), let this melt and become very hot. Crack the eggs, put them either into a cup or on a saucer so that you can make sure they are good, then carefully slide them into the hot fat. Cook for about three minutes, until the white looks quite set. Slip your fish slice under each egg, drain for a second over the pan, then transfer to the hot plates. Serve at once.

To GRILL BACON AND EGGS. Many makers of electric cookers suggest grilling, rather than frying, bacon and egg. Heat the grill on *full* for about 2 minutes. Put the bacon rashers and rinds on the grid over the grill pan and cook rapidly for about 3 minutes, until the bacon is just beginning to curl at the edges. Transfer to hot plates. Remove the grid, but put the grill pan under the heat again for a minute to make sure the fat that has dropped through from the bacon and rinds is very hot. Slide in the eggs (as though into a frying-pan), put under the grill, turning the heat to low, and cook for about 4 minutes until just set.

Note. If fried or grilled eggs habitually break when you try to remove them from the pan, it is fairly obvious the fat is not hot enough.

Main Meal of the Day (Lunch or Dinner)

Stewed Rabbit (white or brown)
Boiled Potatoes with Chopped Parsley.[1]   *Mashed Swedes*[2]
Dumplings (if liked)
Orange Marmalade Sponge Pudding

[1] *See* Vegetable table, p 41.   [2] *See* Vegetable table, p 41.

75

1. Put rabbit to soak for an hour before cooking.
2. Prepare the vegetables for the rabbit and the potatoes and swedes.
3. Put on rabbit to cook.
4. Make sponge pudding, and put on to cook.
5. Put on water for swedes. When boiling put in swedes.
6. Put on water for potatoes. When boiling put in potatoes.
7. Thicken rabbit stew.
8. Make dumplings, then put marmalade sauce ready for the pudding.
9. Dish up first course.

Stewed Rabbit

1 small rabbit. Seasoning. 3 onions. 3 carrots. 1 oz margarine. Water or stock. To THICKEN: 2 level tablespoonfuls flour. 1 teacup milk or 1½ level tablespoonfuls flour. ½ tablespoonful Bisto. ½ teacup water or stock.

To prepare the rabbit it should be cut into neat pieces. Generally, the butcher does this for you. You will not serve the head, but this can be cooked to provide flavour in the stew. Fill a bowl with cold water, adding about 2 tablespoonfuls vinegar, then put in the rabbit, allowing it to soak for about an hour. This both 'sweetens' and whitens the flesh. When ready to cook heat the margarine in the saucepan, and toss the sliced onions in this. Add the rabbit and carrots (halved) and just enough water to come halfway up. Put in about ½ tablespoonful salt and a good pinch of pepper, then cover with the saucepan lid. Bring the liquid just to the boil. You may find a little 'scum' rises to the top; remove this with a spoon. Replace the lid, lower the heat, and allow the rabbit to simmer gently for 1½ hours. Test the flesh with the point of a knife to see that it is quite tender.

WHITE RABBIT STEW OR FRICASSEE

You can keep the carrots in the liquid, but they give a brighter touch of colour if you lift them out and keep them warm. Blend the flour gradually with the cold milk, stir this into the rabbit stock, then bring steadily to the boil, stirring all the time. Cook for about 20 minutes. Dish the rabbit and liquid onto a hot dish, arrange the halved carrots round, with the dumplings, if you are having these as well.

Brown Rabbit Stew

Blend Bisto and flour with the water or stock and continue as before.

Note. Having thickened the stock it is advisable to taste it, for it will need a little extra salt and pepper.

Dumplings

4 oz flour (with plain flour use 1 teaspoonful baking powder). 2 oz shredded suet (margarine could be used, but is not as good). Good pinch salt. Water to mix.

If using shredded suet add this, together with the salt, to the flour. If using butcher's suet either chop it finely or grate on a coarse grater. Margarine must be rubbed into the flour. Gradually stir enough water into the mixture to make a firm dough that you can just gather together with your fingers. (Don't moisten dumpling mixture before you are ready to cook them.) Flour your hands lightly, then roll the mixture into small balls. Look at the rabbit or meat stew, make sure the gravy is boiling and that there is plenty of it, for dumplings tend to absorb a lot of liquid in cooking. If necessary add more water or stock, stir into the gravy, bring to the boil, drop in the dumplings. Cook steadily for about 15 minutes. You can put the lid on the pan.

Savoury Dumplings

Use the dumpling recipe as above, but add about a tablespoonful finely chopped parsley, and a pinch mixed herbs to flavour. These are particularly recommended with rabbit to give additional flavour.

Mashed Swedes

Boil the swedes as directions in the table on p 41. When quite cooked mash with a fork and add a good knob of margarine, pinch pepper – and a pinch nutmeg if liked.

Orange Marmalade Sponge

4 oz flour (with plain flour use 1 teaspoonful baking powder). 2–3 oz margarine. 2–3 oz sugar. 1 egg. Little milk. 2 table-spoonfuls marmalade.

77

This is the way to make all sponge puddings. Flavour them as required with jam or golden syrup at the bottom of the basin instead of marmalade.

Put the marmalade at the bottom of a greased basin (about 1½ pint size). Half-fill a saucepan with water and heat this steadily. Cut the margarine into fairly small pieces, put into a mixing bowl with the sugar, and beat thoroughly with a wooden spoon until it begins to soften, then until the mixture turns whiter. If the margarine is very hard you can warm the bowl slightly before creaming the fat and sugar, but *don't* warm the margarine until it turns into an oil. Break the egg into a cup, beat it lightly, then gradually stir into the margarine. Lastly stir in the flour and just enough milk to make a soft consistency, ie, so that it will drop easily from the spoon. Put on top of the marmalade, leaving plenty of space in the basin for it to rise. Grease a piece of grease-proof paper well. Put the greasy side downwards over the basin, then tuck in the edges tightly. With a little practice you'll soon find you get a neat cover. Nowadays it is considered unnecessary to use pudding cloths. Stand the pudding in a steamer, and having made certain the water in the saucepan is boiling, stand the steamer over this. Cover with a lid and steam for 1¼–1½ hours. During cooking time the water will evaporate. Fill up with boiling water. Steam rapidly for the first ¾ hour, after which the heat can be reduced slightly. If you don't possess a steamer put the basin into a saucepan of boiling water with the water coming halfway up the basin.

Orange Sauce. For a sauce to accompany the pudding, put 2 tablespoonfuls marmalade, 2 tablespoonfuls water, and the grated rind and juice of an orange into a saucepan. Bring to the boil and cook for several minutes. Add a teaspoonful sugar if wished.

Variation

Chocolate Sponge Pudding. Instead of 4 oz flour use 3 oz flour and 1 oz cocoa or chocolate powder. Put into greased basin without jam at the bottom. Serve with chocolate sauce.

Chocolate Sauce. *1½ level dessertspoonfuls chocolate powder or cocoa (the latter makes a more strongly flavoured sauce). 1½ level dessertspoonfuls cornflour. ½–1 tablespoonful sugar. ½ pint milk. Small knob margarine (about size of acorn).*

78

Put the cornflour and chocolate powder into a basin, then stir in a little cold milk, making sure the mixture is very smooth. Put the rest of the milk and sugar into a saucepan, bring to the boil, then pour over the chocolate mixture. Return to the saucepan with the margarine, and cook steadily until thickened and smooth, stirring all the time. To keep the sauce hot without its becoming too thick or sticking to the saucepan, transfer it to a basin or sauceboat and stand this either in another tier of the steamer over the pudding, or on a plate over a pan of boiling water, or in a very low oven.

Light Lunch or Supper
Durham Cutlets with Fried Tomatoes

8 oz cooked meat, minced or finely chopped. 1 oz margarine. 1 oz flour. ¼ pint gravy, stock, or water flavoured with a little Marmite or Bovril. Salt, pepper, mustard, pinch mixed herbs. Tablespoonful chopped parsley. 1 teacup breadcrumbs. To COAT THE CUTLETS: *Crisp breadcrumbs. 1 egg.*

Heat the margarine in a saucepan; you can if you wish fry about a tablespoonful chopped onion in this to give additional flavour. Stir in the flour, away from the heat, and cook the roux for about 5 minutes, until it begins to turn slightly brown. Don't let it burn. Remove pan from the heat, then gradually stir in the gravy or stock. Bring to the boil and cook, stirring well until it is a thick sauce. Add seasoning, parsley, meat, and breadcrumbs. Let the mixture cool, turn out of the saucepan, and form into about 4 cutlet shapes. Beat the egg on a flat plate, then, using a pastry brush, coat the outside of the cutlets with the egg. Put about 2 tablespoonfuls crisp breadcrumbs (or raspings) in a piece of greaseproof paper and turn the cutlets round in this gently until they are completely covered with the crumbs. Pat the crumbs well into the cutlets so that they do not drop off in cooking, then shake each cutlet well to get rid of surplus crumbs. Heat about 2 oz dripping or lard in a frying-pan, put in the cutlets, fry steadily for about 4 minutes to crisp and brown the underside, then turn with a knife and cook for the same time on second side. Lower the heat and allow a further 4 minutes to make sure they are heated right through to the middle. To drain lift onto crumpled tissue paper on a hot dish for about 2 minutes, then transfer to hot plates or another dish, garnished with parsley and the fried tomatoes.

Fried Tomatoes

Halve tomatoes, dusting the tops with a very little salt and pepper. Put into hot fat and cook steadily for about 5 minutes. They do not need turning. If there is room in the frying-pan you can put the tomatoes in with the cutlets, five minutes before dishing-up time.

Grilling the Cutlets and Tomatoes. Both the cutlets and tomatoes could be cooked under the grill. Arrange the tomatoes in the grill pan, dusting with a little salt and pepper, and a scraping of margarine on each half. Put the grid over and lay the cutlets on this, again putting a little margarine on top. Cook quickly for about 4 minutes, turn, add more margarine, cook quickly for the same time, then lower the grill for a further 4–5 minutes.

February Shopping

This month differs little from January, though there are slight variations in the vegetable and fish supplies.

FOODS IN SEASON

Eggs should be even more plentiful, but this is not the month for preserving for the price may drop a little more during March and April (*see* Egg Preserving, p 92).

Fish. It is fairly certain there will still be high seas, and therefore some shortage of fish. Plaice may still be rather poor – watery and full of roe – which means it is wasteful to buy them at this time of the year. WHITE FISH. The same varieties as January, but whiting becomes better this month. OILY FISH. It is advisable not to buy herrings for they are heavy with roe, and their flavour poor. Sprats, trout, whitebait are the best varieties. SHELLFISH. Crayfish, oysters, scallops, shrimps.

Meat. All varieties of meat should be plentiful. During February and for the next few months wood pigeons may be bought at a reasonable price. These can be braised in exactly the same way as Braised Beef (p 125) and served with mixed vegetables. It is advisable to cut the pigeons into halves and cook them for about 2½ hours to make sure they are tender.

Fruit. The first imports of fruit from South Africa generally arrive this month – grapes, peaches, nectarines, and plums. Because they are the first supplies they are rather expensive, so it is advisable to wait a little before buying them.

Vegetables. Much the same varieties as in January, except that celery, celeriac, brussels sprouts are all becoming less plentiful and therefore more expensive.

February Meals

FEBRUARY FIRST

Breakfast
Cereal
Scrambled Eggs on Toast
etc

Scrambled Eggs on Toast

Allow 1 egg per person or for more generous helping 3 eggs for 2 people. Beat the eggs lightly, adding a good pinch salt and pepper. I like about a dessertspoonful milk for each egg, but some people prefer a firmer mixture with no milk added. As the eggs cook very quickly, and spoil if kept waiting, prepare the toast, butter this while hot, and keep hot. Heat a piece of margarine the size of a small walnut in a saucepan, pour in the eggs, cook quickly, stirring well from the bottom until the mixture starts to thicken. Turn the heat very low and continue cooking until as firm as you like. Put on the hot toast, garnish with a small sprig of parsley or slice of tomato (heated under the grill).

Main Meal of the Day (Lunch or Dinner)
Potato Soup
Fried Liver and Bacon
Fried Tomatoes, and/or Onions.   Sauté Potatoes
Green Salad
Coffee Cornflour Mould

1. Make Coffee Cornflour Mould so that it will be cold for the meal.
2. Prepare Green Salad, then potato soup, keeping hot on low heat.
3. If using one frying-pan only cook sauté potatoes, drain, and keep hot.
4. Fry liver, keep hot.
5. Fry onions, then tomatoes.
6. Lastly fry bacon, and make gravy in the frying-pan.

Potato Soup

1 lb potatoes, peeled and halved. 1–2 oz margarine (unless you are using a rather fatty stock, when only about ½ oz should be used). ½ pint milk. 1 pint water or stock. 1 onion. 2 small pieces of celery – when possible. Salt, pepper, celery salt (if not using real celery). Chopped parsley.

Melt the margarine in a saucepan, and toss the sliced onion in this for a few minutes – do not brown. Add the chopped celery, potatoes, water or stock, and seasoning. Bring to the boil, lower the heat, and simmer gently for about 35–40 minutes. Either rub through a hair sieve or beat well, first with a wooden spoon then with a whisk until smooth. Add the milk, bring just to the boil, taste, and re-season if necessary. Pour into hot soup dishes or a soup tureen and garnish with chopped parsley, just before serving.

Green Salad to accompany a hot dish. As the meal consists of rather a lot of fried foods you will find it gives it a 'fresh' taste if you serve a green salad rather than a cooked vegetable. This need consist only of lettuce, watercress, or mustard and cress – with perhaps a French dressing. If you are not frying tomatoes, slices can be arranged on the salad. Put the salads on small plates by each place when serving the liver, etc.

Fried Liver and Bacon

Add a good pinch salt and pepper to about a level tablespoonful flour. Dip each slice of liver in this, shaking off any surplus flour. Heat about 2 oz lard or dripping in the pan (this should be enough for the liver and perhaps the onions too).

Cook steadily for 2–3 minutes, turn and cook for the same time. Don't overcook liver, otherwise it becomes hard. Arrange on a hot dish, and keep hot. Cook the bacon at the last minute as directed on p 75.

Fried Tomatoes and Onions

Since tomatoes are a watery food it is advisable to fry onions first. Cut the peeled onions into thin slices, drying them well in old clean cloth. Dust lightly with a very little flour. Make sure the fat is very hot, put in the onions, and cook until tender and turning golden coloured. Drain on a hot dish covered with crumpled tissue paper, then transfer to second dish with liver at the last minute. Add tomatoes to pan when onions are nearly cooked and cook as directed on p 80.

Sauté Potatoes

Cut cooked potatoes (boiled as directions in Vegetable table, p 41) into large neat pieces. Put into hot fat in the frying-pan – you will need at least 1 oz lard or dripping – and fry until golden coloured and crisp on the outside. Drain on a hot dish covered with crumpled tissue paper, and keep hot in the oven.

Coffee Cornflour Mould

1¼ oz cornflour (2½ level tablespoonfuls). ½ pint milk. ½ pint strong coffee. 1–2 oz sugar. Few drops vanilla essence. About ½ oz butter or margarine (not essential).

Blend the cornflour with a little cold milk. Put the rest of the milk, coffee, vanilla, and sugar into a saucepan and bring just to the boil. Pour steadily over the cornflour, stirring all the time. Return to the pan with the margarine and cook steadily until thick. You must continue to stir all the time otherwise it will become lumpy. Pour into a basin or mould rinsed out in cold water; this enables you to turn it out easily. Put a plate on top so that a skin does not form, and leave in the coolest place possible. Don't put into the refrigerator until cooled slightly. Turn out and serve with cream or the top of the milk. You could decorate with a few cherries.

Variations

Use all milk instead of ½ milk and ½ coffee. Add flavourings to taste. You can also serve with jam or fruit.

Light Lunch or Supper

Macaroni Cheese
Salad or green vegetable

Macaroni Cheese

3 oz macaroni. ½ pint cheese sauce.[1] 2 oz grated cheese (or a little less). 1 tablespoonful crisp breadcrumbs. 1 oz margarine.

Put the macaroni into about 1½ pints boiling water, to which you have added a level teaspoonful salt. Cook steadily until the macaroni is just tender. It is impossible to give exact timing since there are now 'Quick' macaroni cereals available, but it is essential not to overcook, otherwise it is sticky. Test frequently – no macaroni will take longer than 12 minutes. Drain in a colander, arrange it in a hot dish, and pour the cheese sauce over it. Sprinkle cheese and breadcrumbs on top and put the margarine on in several small pieces. Either bake for about 25 minutes near the top of a moderate to moderately hot oven, Mark 5–6 or 375–400 deg. F., until crisp and brown, or put under a hot grill. *Note*. This is a dish that can be prepared during the day and re-heated for an evening meal. If doing this, however, you must make the sauce a little thinner by using ¾ pint of milk instead of ½ pint, for it thickens with standing in the dish with the macaroni.

FEBRUARY SECOND

Breakfast

Fruit Juice
Bacon and Sausages
etc

Fruit Juice

Unless using tinned fruit juices – which are very good – squeeze oranges or grapefruit over squeezer, then pour juice into small tumblers, adding sugar if wished. You can do this overnight to save time in the morning.

Bacon and Sausages

Although in some ways it is a good idea to cook the bacon first so that you get the fat out, and use this for cooking the sausages, bacon should not be kept waiting longer, after it is cooked, than

[1] As for Cauliflower au Gratin, p 74.

is necessary. Sausages take more time to cook than bacon, so this is the method I suggest. Cut the rinds from the rashers of bacon, put into a pan with about $\frac{1}{2}$ oz lard or dripping, and cook quickly until the bottom of the pan is covered with fat. Prick the sausages with a fork to prevent their splitting. Do this gently. Lay sausages in the pan and cook steadily on one side for about 5 minutes, turn over and cook for the same length of time. By this time they should be nicely brown on the outside, but it is essential to see they are *well cooked*, so lower the heat for a further few minutes. Drain with fish slice and put onto hot plates or a hot dish. Put in the rashers of bacon and cook as directed on p 75.

Main Meal of the Day (Lunch or Dinner)

Roast Beef
Yorkshire Pudding   Horseradish Sauce
Roast Potatoes   Roast Parsnips   Cabbage Greens[1]
Apple Pie

PLAN OF WORK

1. Make the Apple Pie, unless this has been cooked the day before, when it will only need warming.
2. Make Yorkshire Pudding.
3. Make Horseradish Sauce.
4. Put in meat (the oven should be pre-heated, of course).
5. Put in potatoes and parsnips.
6. Put in uncooked apple pie, and fat for Yorkshire Pudding.
7. Put in batter.
8. Put on water for greens.
9. Put in greens.
10. Dish up meat, potatoes, and parsnips, and make gravy.
11. Dish up greens, Yorkshire Pudding.
12. Lower heat so that apple pie just keeps warm without over-cooking.

Roast Beef

Pieces of beef suitable for roasting are described on p 31. Put the beef into the roasting tin, adding 4 oz dripping or lard as

[1] *See* Vegetable table, p 39.

you have to cook both potatoes and parsnips. Cook for the first 30 minutes at Mark 6–7 or 425–450 deg. F. Then, if the joint is a large one, reduce to Mark 5–6 or 375–400 deg. F. to prevent its getting dried up outside in order to get it done right through. A really hot oven is, however, essential for a Yorkshire Pudding when it first goes in, so if you have reduced the heat turn the oven to Mark 8 for 5 or 10 minutes after pudding is put in (depending on the fierceness of your oven), then reduce again to Mark 5. Never change the position of Yorkshire Pudding while cooking.

Roast Potatoes

These will take 50–60 minutes to cook, depending on the size. Prepare the potatoes, dry them well in a cloth. Take the meat tin out of the oven, balance it carefully, then put the potatoes into the hot fat round the meat. Turn them with two spoons so that they become coated in the fat before you return them to the oven.

Roast Parsnips

Cook as roast potatoes.

Yorkshire Pudding

4 oz plain flour. Good pinch salt. 1 egg. ½ pint liquid, two-thirds milk and one-third water. Knob of fat, size of a walnut.

Sieve flour and salt together into a basin, drop in the egg, then beat mixture well. Gradually beat in just enough liquid to make a stiff batter. Beat until smooth, leave for about 5 minutes, then gradually beat in the rest of the liquid. A batter like this can be left for some time before being cooked. Keep it in the coolest place possible. When ready to cook, put a knob of lard or dripping into a Yorkshire pudding tin (measuring about 7 inches by 5 inches) and heat in oven for a few minutes. Pour in the batter and cook for about 30 minutes in a hot oven; in every type of cooker use the top of the oven, which is the hottest position. To save cooking time you can cook the batter in small patty tins. Put a piece of fat – the size of a large pea – in each tin, heat this, then pour in the batter and cook for about 15–20 minutes at the top of a hot oven.

Horseradish Sauce

½ pint white sauce.[1] 2 heaped tablespoonfuls freshly grated horse-radish. 1 dessertspoonful vinegar. Good pinch salt, pepper, and sugar.

Wash some fresh horseradish, scrape the outside, rub against moderately coarse grater. Stir the horseradish into the hot sauce, then allow to simmer for 10 minutes. Cool slightly, then whisk in vinegar and seasonings. Any grated horseradish left over can be stored in jars.

Note. There are many excellent horseradish creams and sauces to be bought, which will save the bother of preparing at home; or instead of Horseradish Sauce you can prepare Horseradish Cream.

Horseradish Cream

1 tablespoonful grated horseradish. 2–3 tablespoonfuls cream. ½ teaspoonful vinegar. Seasoning.

Mix all together. This cream is very strong.

Apple Pie

1 lb cooking apples. 2 tablespoonfuls sugar. 4–6 cloves, if liked. Short-crust pastry made from 6 oz flour.[2]

Peel, core, and slice the apples, and put into a pie dish, filling the dish well to the top, as this helps to support the pastry. Add the sugar, enough water to half cover the fruit, and the cloves (if you are using them). Instead of cloves you may care to add one or two pieces of lemon rind. Put a pie support or up-turned egg cup in the middle of the fruit to hold the pastry up. Roll out the pastry into a shape that will easily cover the top of the dish. Cut strips from the edges. Moisten the rim of the pie dish with a little water, arrange the strips of pastry on this. Cover with the pastry lid, then press the top pastry firmly against the first pastry rim. Decorate the edges with fluting, or by pressing down with a fork. Stand the pie dish on a baking sheet, so that there is no risk of juice boiling out and burning in the oven. Bake in the centre of a hot oven, Mark 6–7 or 425–450 deg. F., for about 35 minutes. If the pie seems to be cooking rather quickly reduce the heat, for it is essential to take at least the 35 minutes so that the apples

[1] *See p 74.*   [2] *See p 65.*

are well cooked. If you feel worried about cooking meat, York-shire pudding, and pie together, get the pie cooked either earlier in the day or the day beforehand and re-heat it gently by putting into the oven just before dishing up the first course.

Light Lunch or Supper

Cold Meat
Jacket, or baked, Potatoes
Beetroot Salad

Jacket Potatoes

Allow one good-sized potato for each person. Wash and brush the potatoes well, then dry in a cloth. Cook in a moderate oven, Mark 4–5, or 350–375 deg. F., for 1–1¼ hours. To make the potatoes 'floury', split with a knife and wrap in a clean cloth tightly for about 3 minutes. Put into vegetable dish and serve with a good knob of margarine.

Beetroot Salad

Peel the cooked beetroot and cut into neat slices. Put into a dish, and sprinkle with salt and pepper. If everyone likes vinegar, pour over just enough to cover. Allow to stand for about 30 minutes, and decorate edge of dish with sprigs of watercress.

FEBRUARY THIRD

Breakfast

Porridge[1]
Herring Roes on Toast
etc

Herring Roes on Toast

Although fresh herrings are not at their best this month, you often find plentiful supplies of roes, fresh or frozen. They form an excellent dish for breakfast or supper. Cook in one of the following ways. 1. After washing, put onto a plate with a good knob of margarine, a little milk, and seasoning. Cover with a second plate and steam for about 15 minutes over a pan of boiling water. This keeps the roes moist and whole, but is rather slow

[1] *See* p 60.

for breakfast, so you may prefer to fry them. 2. Wash and dry the roes, then flour lightly. Heat about 2 oz margarine in a pan and cook until golden coloured. 3. Cook in a saucepan in a little milk, until just soft. Season well.

When the roes are cooked put onto hot buttered toast and dust on top with paprika pepper.

Main Meal of the Day (Lunch or Dinner)

Artichoke Soup
— Shepherd's Pie (or Potato Pie)
Celeriac or Turnips[1]
Rhubarb Amber

PLAN OF WORK

1. Prepare vegetables, ie, potatoes, artichokes, celeriac.
2. Make Artichoke Soup, re-heat when desired.
3. Prepare Rhubarb Amber, by cooking fruit, etc.
4. Cook potatoes.
5. Make meat filling for Shepherd's Pie, put on celeriac to cook.
6. Mash potatoes, pile on top, then bake in oven.
7. Complete Rhubarb Amber, make sauce for celeriac if having this.
8. Re-heat soup, put meringue into oven just before dishing up first course.

Artichoke Soup

Use the same recipe as for Potato Soup on p 82, substituting Jerusalem artichokes for potatoes. Follow hints in Vegetable table to keep the artichokes a good colour.

Shepherd's Pie

1½ lb mashed potatoes – a little less could be used if the family are small potato eaters. ¾ lb cooked meat. ¼–½ pint gravy, or stock, or water flavoured with Marmite or Bovril. ½ large onion. Good pinch mixed herbs. 2 or 3 tomatoes. 1 oz dripping or lard. Seasoning. 1 oz margarine.

Cut the cooked meat into small pieces. Heat the dripping in a pan and fry the sliced onion and tomato until tender. Add the meat, stock, seasoning, and mixed herbs. Vary the amount of

[1] See Vegetable table, pp 39 and 41.

89

stock according to personal taste. Pour this into the bottom of a pie dish. Mash the potatoes according to directions on p 72, and when they are very soft and smooth pile on top of the meat mixture. Fork into an attractive shape. Later on, when you are more used to cooking, use a large potato pipe and a cloth piping bag, then you can get a most attractive design. Put the margarine in tiny pieces over the potato, and bake in the centre of a moderately hot oven for 30 minutes until the top is crisp and brown. If both meat filling and potatoes are very hot this dish will only need browning under a hot grill or near the top of a hot oven.

Celeriac or Turnips

Cook whichever vegetable you prefer as directions on pp 39 and 45. Serve with either melted margarine on top or covered with a cheese sauce, as recipe on p 73.

Rhubarb Amber

½ *lb rhubarb. 2 eggs. 1 oz margarine. 3 oz sugar. Approx.* ¼ *teacup water. 2 or 3 glacé cherries.*

To make a more substantial sweet you can use: *1 teacup fine cake or breadcrumbs. Small amount of pastry.*

Put the rhubarb, 1 oz sugar, and about ¼ teacup of water into a saucepan and cook steadily until the rhubarb is soft. Beat mixture until smooth. Add the margarine and the beaten egg yolks. If using cake crumbs also stir these into the fruit mixture.

Line just the edge of a pie dish if you are using pastry, then pour in the fruit mixture. Set for about 25 minutes in a moderately hot oven. Beat the egg whites until very stiff, fold in nearly all the sugar. Pile on top of the rhubarb mixture, put pieces of cherry on top, and set the meringue for about 15 minutes in a very moderate oven, Mark 3–4 or 325–350 deg. F. As this sweet is much nicer hot than cold there is no need to set the meringue very slowly. I suggest you put it into the oven to set meringue just as you dish up first course.

Variations

Apple Amber. Use apples instead of rhubarb (1 lb fruit when peeled and cored). Add a little lemon juice to flavour.

Gooseberry Amber. If wished the cooked fruit can be put through a sieve, to remove the pips.

Plum Amber. Stone fruit after or before cooking, flavour with few drops almond essence.

Light Lunch or Supper

Cheese and Tomato Soufflé

Cheese and Tomato Soufflé

1 oz margarine. 1 oz flour. ¼ pint milk. 2 or 3 tomatoes. Seasoning. Yolks of 3 and whites of 4 eggs. 2–3 oz grated cheese.

If you haven't a proper soufflé dish, then use a straight-sided casserole. It should hold about 2 pints. Grease this with margarine and arrange the thinly sliced tomatoes over the bottom. Heat margarine in a saucepan, then stir in the flour, away from the heat. Return to heat again and cook the roux gently for about 3 minutes. Add the cold milk – again away from heat – stirring all the time. Cook steadily until a thick sauce, cool slightly, then stir in the beaten egg yolks, cheese, and seasoning, including a good pinch mustard. Whisk the egg whites until very stiff, then *fold* them gently into the mixture. This isn't difficult to do if you use a palette knife or metal spoon, but do not be rough, otherwise you lose the lightness of the eggs. Pour into the dish, about half filling it. Bake for about 25–30 minutes in the centre of a moderate to hot oven, Mark 5–6 or 375–400 deg. F. Bring out of the oven and serve at once. The tomatoes can be omitted if wished.

Variations

Fish. Use about 4 oz flaked, cooked fish instead of cheese.

Ham. Use about 4 oz minced or finely chopped cooked ham instead of cheese.

Mushrooms. Fry gently about 4 oz mushrooms, chop finely, and add to mixture in place of cheese.

Spinach. Stir about a teacup cooked sieved spinach into milk mixture instead of cheese. Or you can use both spinach and cheese.

Remember:

1. Fold egg whites in gently.
2. Bake as soon as mixed.
3. Serve as soon as baked.

March Shopping

With the promise of better weather most people begin to want lighter food. This month, therefore, try to mix plenty of fresh green salads and fruit with your 'cold weather' fare.

FOODS IN SEASON

Eggs should be at their cheapest and best, so it is well worth while preserving a few for late autumn and winter (*see* below).

Fish. If the weather is becoming more temperate you should find all fish cheaper, and a more plentiful variety available. WHITE FISH. Cod, haddock, hake, halibut, skate, sole, turbot. OILY FISH. Salmon, sprats, trout, whitebait. SHELLFISH. Crayfish, prawns, scallops, shrimps.

Fruit. South African fruits are generally at their cheapest which means it is sometimes possible to have luxury fruits like grapes, pineapple, peaches, and nectarines. Include a little fruit in your green salads, eg, sliced apple, pineapple, oranges, bananas.

Meat. As for February (p 80).

Vegetables. Much depends on the weather, which can vary so much at this time of the year. If it is good then many varieties of greens can be obtained, and cheaply, too. Use shredded cabbage, spring greens, etc, in salads in place of lettuce, for this is still inclined to lack flavour. GREEN VEGETABLES. Brussels sprouts (though these are rather wasteful for they are now rather open), cabbage and cabbage greens, cauliflower, kale, mushrooms, savoys. ROOT VEGETABLES. Carrots, both old and new (though latter scarce and therefore expensive), leeks (particularly good), onions, swedes, turnips.

To Preserve Eggs

If you have space to store a preserving pail, then keep the eggs in this, using a waterglass (or isinglass) solution. You can buy special egg-preserving pails, with lids and a metal 'basket' which enables you to lower the eggs into the solution easily. A covered zinc pail with a lid can easily be used, or an earthenware crock. You must have a lid to prevent the solution evaporating, and it is essential to store the pail in a cool dry place.

PRESERVING IN WATERGLASS. You buy the solution in tins from ironmongers, chemists, and grocers. Dilute it with water according to the directions on the tin. Never try to economize by using more water than stated. 'Shop' eggs can be used, but you will get better results by using new-laid eggs that are between 12 and 24 hours old. Make quite certain the eggs are not cracked. Lower them carefully into the solution. You can add eggs as and when you wish, there is no need to fill the pail at one time. *To cook preserved eggs.* Take the eggs carefully out of the pail and wash away the waterglass under cold water. For frying, poaching, scrambling, and general cooking the eggs can be broken and used in the usual way. Before boiling an egg preserved in waterglass prick it in about three places with a sewing needle. This prevents the eggshell cracking badly.

It is generally found that eggs keep perfectly for about nine months.

COATING THE EGGS. For many years there have been preparations on the market for coating eggs but these now seem to be less plentiful. If you have difficulty in obtaining them you can spread Vaseline over the eggs. If using the commercial coating follow the directions carefully. You can use these eggs for all cooking purposes, and I have never found it necessary to prick the shells for boiling, although this can be done as a precaution against cracking.

March Meals

MARCH FIRST

Breakfast

Cereal
Fish Cakes
etc

Fish Cakes

$\frac{1}{2}$ *lb mashed potatoes. 1 lb cooked fish. 1 egg. Salt, pepper.*
For coating: *1 egg. Flour. Crisp breadcrumbs. 2 oz lard.*
Naturally if serving fish cakes for breakfast you must cook both potatoes and fish the day before, and it is advisable to prepare the fish cakes completely so that they only need frying in the

morning. Put into a basin the potatoes, mashed as directions on
p 72, and the fish (cod, hake, or other white fish) cooked as
directions on p 99. Mix thoroughly with a fork. Add the beaten
egg, salt, and pepper. Form into about 8 flat cakes. Roll these
cakes in a little flour, then brush lightly with beaten egg and coat
with breadcrumbs, as described on p 117.

Heat the fat in the frying-pan and when a faint haze is seen
fry quickly on one side, turn and fry again on the other side.
Drain on crumpled tissue paper for about 2 minutes and serve
at once.

Note. To be more economical you could use ½ an egg in mixing
the fish cakes and the other half for brushing them on the outside. When you serve fish cakes for a supper dish have tomatoes
and peas with them.

Main Meal of the Day (Lunch or Dinner)

Boiled Brisket of Beef
Carrots   Turnips
Boiled Potatoes
Brigade Pudding, or Apple and Fruit Layer Pudding

PLAN OF WORK

1. Soak the meat very early if this was not done overnight.
2. Put on brisket to cook, with prepared vegetables.
3. Make pudding and put on to cook.
4. Prepare rest of vegetables if this was not completed earlier.
5. Put on water for carrots, turnips, and potatoes – to save saucepans they can all be cooked together.

Brisket of Beef

*Piece of beef, about 3–4 lb. 4 small onions. 4 small carrots. Good
pinch pepper, mustard.*

It is a good idea to buy enough brisket to allow for a cold meal,
for it is delicious with salad. Soak the beef in *cold* water for an
hour or two. If the butcher says it is very salt soak overnight.
Put the beef into a large saucepan with the vegetables, and half
cover with cold water. Add a good pinch pepper and mustard.
Bring quickly to the boil. Remove any scum that comes to the
top. Put the lid on the saucepan, lower the heat, and simmer
gently – allowing about 30 minutes to each lb and 30 minutes over,

ie, a piece 4 lb will take $2\frac{1}{2}$ hours to cook. If wished, dumplings can be cooked with this, allowing them about 15 minutes quick cooking (*see* p 77). Do not thicken the liquid. To serve the meat put it on to a large, hot dish, with the vegetables and stock round, then garnish with dumplings and a few of the freshly cooked vegetables.

Boiled Carrots, Turnips, and Potatoes

Directions for cooking these separately are on pp 39 and 41, but they can be cooked together to save saucepans. Keep the potatoes rather large, so that they do not break while the firmer carrots and turnips are cooking.

As you will see below it is suggested that extra root vegetables are cooked and turned into a Russian salad for a supper dish.

Brigade Pudding

$\frac{3}{4}$ *lb cooking apples, peeled and cored. 1 oz sugar. Pinch mixed spice. 2–3 oz dried fruit.*

FOR THE PASTRY. *6 oz flour (with plain flour 1 teaspoonful baking powder). Good pinch salt. 3 oz shredded suet. Water to mix.*

Slice the apples very thinly.

To make the suet pastry. Sieve salt and baking powder into the flour (if using plain flour), add the suet and enough water to make a firm dough. Roll out to just over $\frac{1}{4}$ inch thick, then cut into 4 rounds, one very small and the size of the bottom of the basin and three others each one a little larger than the last. Grease a $1\frac{1}{2}$ pint basin, put in the bottom layer, then cover with some of the sliced apples, sprinkling of sugar, dried fruit, and spice. Fill the basin like this, ending with a layer of pastry. Cover with greased paper (*see* directions under Sponge Pudding, p 78). Put into a steamer and cook for 2 hours, filling with boiling water as the saucepan becomes drier. Serve with custard sauce – made as directed on the packet of custard powder. To keep hot while you have the first course turn into sauceboat or basin and stand over hot water.

Light Lunch or Supper

Cold Brisket or other Meat
Russian Salad   Green Salad

Serve the meat on a dish garnished with rings of tomato, lettuce, etc.

Russian Salad

Dice as many root vegetables as possible. In summer left-over peas and beans can be added to the salad. Toss in mayonnaise, pile into dish, garnish with sprigs of watercress and chopped parsley.

MARCH SECOND

Breakfast

Fruit Juice[1]
Bacon and Fried Bread
etc

Bacon and Fried Bread

First cook bacon[2] and bacon rinds to get as much fat out as possible. Keep bacon hot without overcooking. Put in a piece of bread for each person, cook rapidly until crisp and brown on underside, turn and cook on the second side. Drain on fish slice for a minute, then serve at once.

Main Meal of the Day (Lunch or Dinner)

Meat Curry, with Chutney   Boiled Rice
Cabbage tossed in Margarine[3]
Pancakes and Lemon

PLAN OF WORK

1. Make the curry sauce – do not put in meat if this is already cooked.
2. Make the pancake batter.
3. Put on water for rice; when boiling put on rice. Put meat into curry.
4. Drain rice, wash to separate grains, and re-heat.
5. Put on water for cabbage; when boiling put on cabbage.
6. Cook pancakes and keep hot on hot dish.
7. Dish up first course.

Meat Curry

FOR THE CURRY SAUCE. *1–2 oz margarine or good dripping. 1 small onion. 1 small apple. $\frac{1}{2}$–1 tablespoonful curry powder. 1*

[1] *See* p 84.   [2] *See* p 75.   [3] *See* Vegetable table, p 39.

tablespoonful flour. 1 tablespoonful dried fruit. 1 dessertspoonful dessicated coconut. 1 teaspoonful sugar. 1 dessertspoonful chutney. Pinch nutmeg, turmeric.[1] Salt, pepper, mustard. Squeeze of lemon juice. 1 pint stock or water.

You may feel alarmed at the long list of ingredients for the curry sauce, but naturally some of the less essential, ie, the spices, coconut, and turmeric could be omitted, though they help to give good flavour. Peel and slice the apple and onion. Heat the fat in a pan and fry the onion and apple until soft, then work in the curry powder, paste, and flour. Cook this 'roux' for several minutes, then gradually blend in the stock or water. Bring to the boil and cook until thickened. Add other ingredients, then allow to *simmer gently* for several hours if possible. The longer the sauce cooks the better, but it must cook slowly so that there is no danger of its burning. Cooked meat, neatly diced, should be added about 20 minutes before serving.

Serve the curry piled on the boiled rice (*see* below) and with a dish of chutney. You may also like to serve a small dish of sliced tomatoes and another of sliced bananas,

Variations

Eggs, hard-boiled. Simmer the whole shelled eggs in the sauce for 10 minutes.

Fish. Use water or fish stock, put in the uncooked fish, and cook gently for about 40 minutes. Prawns or shellfish want only about 15 minutes' cooking in the sauce.

Meat, poultry, or rabbit uncooked. Cut into neat pieces and cook for about 1½ hours in the sauce. You may need to add a little extra liquid so that the sauce is not too thick.

Vegetables. Put the raw root vegetables into the hot sauce and cook steadily for about 25 minutes.

Dried vegetables, lentils in particular, should be cooked for about 1 hour, after soaking in cold water for at least 12 hours.

[1] A yellow powder produced from the tubers of an Indian plant, bought by the ounce from the chemist.

Boiled Rice
for curry

Allow 1 oz rice for each person and $\frac{1}{2}$ pint water at least in which to cook each ounce of rice; plenty of water prevents it sticking. Put the water on to boil, adding 1 teaspoonful salt to each quart of water. When boiling drop in the washed rice and cook rapidly for about 10 minutes until the rice is just firm. Do not overcook, otherwise it becomes too soft. Drain the rice through a fine sieve, then put under the cold water tap to separate the grains. Put the rice on a tea cloth on a dish or baking sheet, and dry in a very slow oven. The extra trouble of rinsing and re-heating is well worth while, for it produces white rice with each grain separate, instead of a rather sticky mass.

Pancakes

Use the same recipe as for Yorkshire Pudding batter (p 86). A second egg improves the pancakes. In addition you require butter or lard for frying, sugar, and lemons. Put a very small amount of butter into the frying pan, so that when melted it just covers the bottom of the pan. Transfer the pancake batter to a jug, for it is easier to pour from there. Pour out just enough to give a very thin covering over the bottom of the pan. Cook rapidly for about two minutes until the pancake is golden brown on the underside, then either toss or turn and cook for the same time on the second side. Turn the pancake onto a piece of sugared greaseproof paper, then roll with the help of a knife. Ideally pancakes should be eaten as soon as they are cooked, but this is rarely possible in a home, so put them on a *hot* dish and keep (uncovered) in a very low oven. Arrange slices of lemon round the dish and dust a little more sugar on top of each pancake. *To toss a pancake.* Hold the pan loosely in your hand, so that the wrist is quite flexible, then flick sharply upwards. At first you will probably find the pancake just 'flops' and doesn't turn in the air, but, provided you've cooked it well on the underside, with a little practice you will soon have good results (*see* Pl. 21).
To turn a pancake. When cooked on the underside slide a broad-bladed knife under the pancake, balance it under the very middle, then turn over carefully.

To remove pancake from pan. Simply turn pan upside down over sugared paper, and the pancake will drop out in one piece.

Light Lunch or Supper

Fish Pie
Cauliflower[1]

Fish Pie

1 lb white fish, an economical variety can be used. 1 lb mashed potatoes. ½ pint anchovy sauce. Seasoning. 1 oz margarine. Parsley.

Put the fish into a pan with about ½ pint water, salt, and pepper, and a bay leaf, if wished. Simmer steadily until just soft, but not broken, otherwise the fish tastes 'watery'. This will only take about 5 minutes if using filleted cod or fresh haddock, or 10 minutes for thicker pieces of fish. Drain the fish well over the pan with your fish slice before putting it onto a plate. Remove any bones and skin with the point of a knife. Using a fork, break the fish into large pieces (this is called flaking) and lay at the bottom of a greased pie dish. Make the anchovy sauce – to do this you will need the ingredients for a white sauce and anchovy essence.

Anchovy Sauce

½ pint white sauce (p 74), to which add 1 small teaspoonful anchovy essence.

As this has a very salt flavour add less salt than usual.

Pour the sauce over the fish, then cover with the mashed potatoes. You can put a few small knobs of margarine on top to encourage the potatoes to brown. Bake for 30 minutes just above the middle of a moderate to moderately hot oven, Mark 5–6 or 375–400 deg. F. This takes about 30–35 minutes – reduce heat if necessary. Garnish with small pieces of parsley.

Variations

Cheese Sauce. *See* p 73.

Egg Sauce. (*a*) When the sauce has thickened take it off the heat for a few minutes so that it is no longer boiling, then add a

[1] *See* Vegetable table, p 39.

whisked egg, and cook slowly *without boiling* for about three minutes. If it boils it will curdle. This sauce is ideal for vegetable or chicken dishes. (*b*) Add chopped hard-boiled egg to the sauce. It looks attractive if the chopped hard-boiled white, or whites, of one or two eggs are stirred into the sauce, then the chopped or sieved yolks are sprinkled over the top.

Prawn or Shrimp Sauce. Add ½–1 teacup chopped shrimps or prawns to the white sauce. Ideal for fish dishes.

MARCH THIRD

Breakfast
Sausages and Apple Rings
Toast, etc

Sausages and Apple Rings
Allow about ½ large cooking apple per person, and 2–3 sausages. Core the apples, wipe the outsides, but do not peel. Cut each apple into about six rings. Cook the sausages as described on p 93. Keep hot, then fry the apples in the remaining hot fat. Allow about 3 minutes, then turn and fry the same time on the other side. Drain well and serve with the sausages. The 'bite' of these apple rings makes a complete change with the sausages.

Main Meal of the Day (Lunch or Dinner)
Scotch Broth
Toad in the Hole, with minced meat
Spinach[1]   *Oven 'Fried' Potatoes*
Jam Roll

PLAN OF WORK
1. Make the Scotch Broth and prepare other vegetables.
2. Make the pastry for the Jam Roll, batter for 'toad in hole'.
3. Having pre-heated oven, put in the fat and minced meat.
4. After 5 minutes' cooking, remove dish of fat and meat, and pour over the batter.
5. Return to oven, then put in the jam roll.
6. Put potatoes into oven.

[1] *See* Vegetable table, p 41.

7. Put on spinach.
8. Dish up first course.

Scotch Broth

½–¾ *lb neck of mutton or stewing beef. 1 carrot. 1 small turnip.
1 onion or large leek. 2 pints water. 1 oz pearl barley. Pepper,
salt. 1 tablespoonful chopped parsley (or little less, if preferred).*

Wash the meat, and cut into small pieces. Put in the saucepan,
cover with cold water, add a little seasoning, then the barley.
To give the cereal a better flavour and appearance, blanch it,
by putting it in cold water in a separate saucepan, bringing just
to the boil, then strain off the water. Bring the broth to the boil,
and remove any scum that has come to the top with a metal
spoon. Put the lid on the saucepan, lower the heat, and simmer
steadily for about 2½ hours. The diced vegetables should be put
in after the meat has been cooking for an hour. Before serving,
the meat can be taken out, chopped more finely, then returned
to the broth. Sprinkle the parsley on top of the soup at the last
minute.

Note. Because Scotch Broth is such a filling soup, particularly
if the meat is left in as suggested above and served in the soup,
you can have a lighter main course than usual.

Toad in the Hole

Yorkshire Pudding batter.[1]

FILLING. *4–8 oz minced beef. 1 or 2 sliced tomatoes can be included.
½ oz lard or dripping. Salt, pepper.*

Make the batter and let it stand as long as possible. Put the fat
into the Yorkshire pudding tin, and put this as near the top of
a hot oven, Mark 6–7 or 425–450 deg. F., as possible. Leave for
about 3 minutes, then remove from the oven, put in the meat,
sliced tomatoes, adding seasoning.

Replace the tin in the hot oven, but this time just above the
middle. Cook for about 5 minutes, remove once again, pour over
the batter. Return to the oven and cook for approximately 30
minutes until the batter has risen well and is crisp and brown.
Serve at once. This takes about 30–35 minutes, reduce heat
if necessary.

[1] *See* p 86.

101

Variations

Toad in the Hole can be varied according to the fillings available.

Bacon and Tomato. Put ½ oz fat in the tin. When hot cover bottom of tin with sliced tomatoes and bacon. Cook for 5 minutes, pour the batter over and cook as before.

Cheese. Heat the fat, stir about 2–3 oz grated cheese into the batter. Cook as above.

Cheese and Tomato. Heat the fat, arrange a good layer of sliced tomatoes in this, cooking them for about 3–5 minutes. Pour the batter over them and cook as before.

Mixed Filling. For a special occasion, allow 1 small chop (removing bone from meat), half a small kidney, and 1 tomato for each person. Heat the fat, arrange each portion of meat, etc, in a corner of the tin. Cook for 5 minutes, pour the batter over, and cook as before.

Sausages. This is popular, and the most usual filling. Heat the fat. Prick the sausages gently and cook for 5–10 minutes, according to size. Pour batter over and finish cooking as before.

Oven-fried Potatoes

1 lb potatoes. Salt, pepper. 2 oz fat.

Peel and slice the potatoes. Keep the slices as near the same thickness as possible, so that they all get cooked together. Melt the fat, in a small basin in a pan of hot water. Brush a large baking sheet over with some of the fat. Put the sliced potatoes on this, sprinkling with salt and pepper. Brush the tops with the melted fat. Cook for about 20–25 minutes near the top of a hot oven. This method of cooking gives a crisp potato, easily, and without using an undue amount of fat.

Jam Roll

Short-crust pastry made from 6 oz flour, etc (see p 65). 2 oz jam.

Roll out the pastry until it is a neat oblong, and about ¼ in thick. Spread lightly with jam. Turn in the edges, so that the jam will not come out, then roll up like a Swiss roll. Lift onto a lightly greased baking tin, and bake just below the centre of a hot oven,

Mark 6–7 or 425–450 deg. F., for about 20 minutes. Lower the heat to very moderate to moderate, Mark 4–5 or 350–375 deg. F., and cook for a further 25 minutes.

Note. If cooking with Toad in the Hole, etc, the oven temperature can be reduced about 10 minutes before dishing up first course without spoiling batter or potatoes.

Light Lunch or Supper

Fried Sprats
With lemon and brown bread and butter

Fried Sprats

Allow about 1¼ lb for 3–4 people. Wash and dry the fish, then cut off the heads with kitchen scissors. Put a good tablespoonful flour on a large plate, adding a ½ teaspoonful salt and pinch pepper. Roll the fish in the seasoned flour, shaking off any surplus. Heat about 2 oz fat in a frying-pan, then fry enough sprats to cover the pan until crisp and brown. Drain well, first on the fish slice, then on crumpled tissue paper on a hot dish. Keep hot while frying the next batch. Serve on a large dish, garnished with parsley and slices of lemon.

April Shopping

There should be little or no difficulty in obtaining generous supplies of green vegetables and fish this month. In fact if the weather is good there is an almost unlimited variety of vegetable produce. I should make good use of green vegetables during the next weeks, for as soon as peas, beans, etc, make their appearance most people prefer to serve these.

FOODS IN SEASON

Eggs should be as plentiful as in March, so if the opportunity arises to preserve these do so (*see* p 92).

Fish. This is a good month to include plenty of fish in the menu, for catches should be large, and while the weather is not too hot one is quite sure of fresh fish. Skate is at its best. WHITE FISH.

Cod, hake, haddock, halibut, skate, sole, turbot. OILY FISH. Particularly notable are the first of the mackerel, a delicious fish, which can be cooked in exactly the same way as herrings (*see* p 128). Also available salmon, trout, whitebait. SHELLFISH. Crab, crawfish, crayfish, oysters, prawns, shrimps. Lobster comes into season.

Fruit. Much the same as March, but imports of South African fruit generally more scarce and therefore becoming dearer. First outdoor crops of rhubarb should be available.

Meat. As for February (p 80).

Vegetables. Very much the same as March, but look out for a delicious vegetable, purple sprouting broccoli, rather like tiny cauliflower heads in purple colour. Cook just like ordinary green vegetables.

April Meals

APRIL FIRST

Breakfast

Fruit Juice[1]
Bacon and Potato Cakes
etc

Bacon and Potato Cakes

The potato cakes should be prepared overnight. For these you need:

Approximately ½ lb cooked and mashed potatoes (see p 72). 1 good tablespoonful flour. Salt, pepper. 1 teaspoonful chopped parsley.

Mix nearly all the flour with the potatoes, then add salt, pepper, and parsley. Form into 8 small flat cakes, and dust these with the last of the flour.

Fry the bacon first, and bacon rinds (*see* p 75), keep bacon hot, then quickly fry the potato cakes until they are crisp and brown on bottom side. Turn and cook on the second side.

See p 84.

Main Meal of the Day (Lunch or Dinner)

Boiled Chicken
White or hard-boiled Egg Sauce
New Potatoes[1] or Cream of Potatoes
Purple Sprouting Broccoli
Queen of Puddings

PLAN OF WORK

1. Put on chicken to cook.
2. Prepare vegetables.
3. Cook first part of pudding.
4. Put meringue on pudding. Get water ready for potatoes.
5. Put in potatoes.
6. Put on water for broccoli.
7. Cook broccoli.
8. Make sauce. Dish up first course.

Boiled or Steamed Chicken

Buy a boiling fowl, but make sure you are buying a good fleshy bird. So often the older birds used for boiling tend to be 'all bone and skin', so feel the breast and legs to see if there is plenty of meat. It is far better to steam the bird if possible, for you have both better appearance and flavour. Wash and dry it inside and out, then put into the steamer, sprinkling the top lightly with salt and pepper. Allow 30–40 minutes per lb and 30 minutes over. If you are cooking a bird over 5 lb then 30 minutes a lb should be enough. Under that weight it is advisable to allow 40 minutes. Make sure the water in the saucepan under the steamer boils *hard* all the cooking time. If you wish to boil the fowl – which of course gives an excellent flavoured stock for soups, etc – put the bird into cold water, adding salt and pepper (also an onion, if wished) and cook for the same length of time as above. The water should only boil slightly during cooking period. Dish up onto a hot dish, garnish with parsley, and pour over some of the sauce. Serve the rest of the sauce separately.

White or Hard-Boiled Egg Sauce

Particulars for making these sauces are given on pp 74 and 99. For 4 people allow ½ pint to ¾ pint of sauce, as you have to pour

[1] These will be imported.

some over the bird as well as serving sauce separately. When making the sauce use half milk and half chicken stock if the fowl has been boiled.

Cream of Potatoes

Boil and mash the potatoes as directions on p 72, but instead of adding just milk use about 8–12 tablespoons cream (or milk and cream). The potatoes will be very soft, so hold over a low heat to dry slightly. The mixture should, however, be kept soft and creamy. Dust paprika pepper on top of the potatoes when dished up.

Queen of Puddings

1 teacup cake crumbs, or fine breadcrumbs. 2 tablespoonfuls jam.
2 eggs. ½ pint milk. 3 tablespoonfuls sugar. ½ oz margarine.

Note. You can manage with one egg only, in which case use only 2 tablespoonfuls sugar.

Spread half the jam thinly on bottom of the greased pie dish. Put the crumbs, milk, margarine, and 1 tablespoonful sugar into a saucepan, heat gently, then stir in beaten egg yolks. Pour into pie dish. Bake for 30 minutes in the centre of a very moderate oven, Mark 3–4 or 325–350 deg. F., until the pudding feels fairly firm. Spread the top with jam. Beat egg whites until stiff, fold in nearly all the sugar. Pile on top of the pudding, dusting with sugar. Bake in a very slow oven, Mark 1 or 275 deg. F., for about 40 minutes until the meringue is firm. This pudding is delicious hot or cold.

Light Lunch or Supper

Cold Salmon with Mayonnaise[1] or quick Tartare Sauce
Green Salad[2]   Potato Salad[3]

Cold Steamed Salmon

Fresh salmon is such a delicious fish, and generally so expensive, that it should be cooked with the greatest care. Remember it is very solid and 'filling', so you need not allow quite so much per person as for other fish. The fish should be firm with bright eyes, the flesh pink, the smell not too strong. A cut from the middle of the salmon has the best flavour but is often dearer.

One of the best ways to cook salmon is as follows: choose a saucepan with a tightly fitting lid. Put in the salmon with enough

[1] *See p 69.*   [2] *See p 68.*   [3] *See p 67.*

cold water to cover, and a good pinch salt. If you like the slightly oily texture of salmon wrap the fish in lightly oiled greaseproof paper, seasoning before putting it into the cold water. Bring just to the boil. Put on the lid, remove pan from heat, and leave until cold. In this way there is no danger of overcooking the fish. Drain well, then arrange on dish garnished with rings of cucumber and lettuce.

Tartare Sauce

1 teacup mayonnaise[1]. 2 finely chopped gherkins. 2 teaspoonfuls finely chopped parsley. 1 teaspoonful chopped capers. Squeeze of lemon juice.

Mix all the ingredients together. This is delicious with salmon and should be served separately in a sauceboat.

APRIL SECOND

Breakfast
Cereal
Cod's Roe
etc

Cod's Roe

Allow either 3 oz cooked roe or 4 oz uncooked roe per person. Some fishmongers cook the roe before selling it; you can easily tell the difference, for the uncooked roe is a rather bright pink and very soft, whereas the cooked is paler and firm. If you buy uncooked roe put either into a steamer, sprinkling lightly with salt, or in a small quantity of boiling salted water. Cook steadily for about 10 minutes, then allow to cool. It is advisable to do this overnight if serving for a breakfast dish. Cut the cooked roe into slices. Heat about 1–2 oz fat in a frying-pan and fry on either side until crisp and brown, then serve on toast. You can also fry the roe to serve with bacon.

Main Meal of the Day (Lunch or Dinner)
Chicken Cutlets
Mashed Potatoes[2]   Spring Greens[3]
Chocolate Sponge Pudding, with Chocolate Sauce[4]

[1] *See* p 69.   [2] *See* p 72.   [3] *See* Vegetable table, p 39.   [4] *See* p 78.

1. Prepare sponge pudding, put on to cook.
2. Prepare Chicken Cutlets.
3. Put on water for potatoes, then cook these.
4. Put on water for spring greens and cook these.
5. Fry cutlets, then mash potatoes.
6. Make chocolate sauce, keep warm.
7. Dish up first course.

Chicken Cutlets

Follow the same recipe and method of cooking as for Durham cutlets (p 79), but substitute cooked chicken for the minced meat. The chicken should either be chopped very finely, or put through a mincer. If doing this, you can include the skin as well; there is no need to waste any of the chicken. For this type of dish don't use the breast, but left-over meat from back, wings, etc. If you have any chicken stock use this for making the thick sauce. When serving the cutlets they can be accompanied with a rasher of fried bacon if wished.

Light Lunch or Supper

Chicken Soup
Baked Bean Casserole
'Bubble and Squeak'

Chicken Soup

There are many recipes for Chicken Soup, varying from those that use the whole of a chicken to give flavour. It is safe to assume, however, that in the average family all meat will have been used from the bird, leaving just the bones, some skin perhaps, and maybe the giblets. All of these combined will make a good-flavoured soup. Follow the recipe for Scotch Broth on p 101, using the same vegetables, barley, etc. If you use the giblets the meat can be removed after cooking and chopped finely, then returned to the soup. If you have boiled the chicken the stock will give additional flavour to the soup, otherwise cover the bones, etc, with water and cook as directed in the Scotch Broth recipe.

Baked Bean Casserole

1 large tin baked beans, 2 tomatoes, 2 hard-boiled eggs. 2 table-spoonfuls grated cheese. 1 oz margarine.

Fry sliced tomatoes in the margarine, then mix with the beans. Put half the beans into a dish, then a layer of sliced hard-boiled eggs, then the rest of the beans. Cover the top with cheese and cook near the top of a hot oven for about 20 minutes. If you do not wish to use the oven, heat the beans with the fried tomatoes, slicing the eggs while hot also, and fill the dish as before. Cover with the cheese and brown under a hot grill.

'Bubble and Squeak'

Equal quantities of cooked mashed potatoes and cooked green vegetable (see p 39). Good ounce of lard or dripping.

Mix the potatoes and green vegetable together, mashing thoroughly, and adding additional seasoning if wished. Heat the lard in the frying-pan and spread over the vegetable mixture. Cook steadily until you are sure it is very hot. Slip under your palette knife and fold in half away from the handle. Slide onto a hot dish. If cooked well you have a brown crisp skin to this dish. Although very popular with most people this cannot be termed an ideal method of cooking vegetables, or serving them, since the green vegetable is cooked twice and therefore loses all vitamins.

APRIL THIRD

Breakfast

Oslo Breakfast. This meal – quite different from the usual British breakfast – has been recognized as an ideal start to the day. It consists of bread and butter (preferably wholemeal), fresh fruit and milk, with a little cheese if wished. It is a welcome change, particularly after the winter months.

Main Meal (Lunch or Dinner)

Boiled Bacon
New Carrots[1]   Potatoes   Cabbage
Vanilla Cornflour Mould   Fresh Fruit Jelly

[1] *See* Vegetable table, p 39.

109

1. Make Fruit Jelly. If your larder is hot this could be made the day beforehand.
2. Put on bacon to cook. Make cornflour mould.
3. Prepare vegetables.
4. Put on water for potatoes and carrots.
5. Cook potatoes and carrots.
6. Dish up Boiled Bacon, keep hot.
7. Cook cabbage in the stock.
8. Dish up first course.

Boiled Bacon

The ideal bacon for boiling is back, gammon, and collar. Allow 30 minutes per lb and 30 minutes over. If you think the bacon may be a little salt soak for about 2 hours in cold water.

Put the bacon into cold water. Bring slowly to the boil, then simmer gently. If wished you can add one or two onions to the liquid. When ready to dish up, put on a very hot dish, pouring over about $\frac{1}{2}$ pint of the stock in which it has been cooked. Garnish with the new carrots when they are cooked.

Cabbage in Bacon Stock

Pour away some of the bacon stock (this could be kept for soups), but see you have about 1 inch at the bottom of the pan. Put in the shredded cabbage, only very lightly seasoning this. Cook quickly for about 8 minutes, strain, and serve at once.

Vanilla Cornflour Mould

Follow recipe for Coffee Mould (p 83), using all milk and 1 teaspoonful vanilla essence. When turned out decorate with a tablespoonful jam if wished.

Fresh Fruit Jelly

1 packet flavoured jelly cubes or crystals, preferably lemon. 1 small orange. 1 banana. 1 apple.

Make the jelly, and when cold stir in the fruit. The banana should be sliced, the orange cut into tiny pieces and pith, skin, and pips removed, the apple finely diced. Pour into a mould, rinsed out in cold water, so that the jelly will turn out. Before trying to turn out of the mould, dip the jelly for about ½ minute in a bowl of hot water. Invert over a large plate, and it should slip out easily.

Light Lunch or Supper
Hard-Boiled Egg Cutlets
Green Salad[1]

Hard-Boiled Egg Cutlets

3 or 4 hard-boiled eggs. 1 teacup breadcrumbs. ¼ pint thick panada or white sauce. TO COAT: *Beaten egg. Crisp breadcrumbs.* TO FRY: *2 oz lard or dripping.*

First make the white sauce, as directions on p 74, but using ¼ pint instead of ½ pint milk, as a much thicker sauce is wanted. Stir in the finely chopped eggs and crumbs. Allow mixture to cool, and then form into four cutlet shapes. Brush with beaten egg and dip in crumbs, as on p 117. Heat the fat and fry until crisp and brown on either side. Drain well. Serve hot or cold with the green salad.

May Shopping

This is the month that sees the beginning of the summer vegetables and fruits, but very few of them, and rather expensive, so don't buy them except for special occasions.

FOODS IN SEASON

Eggs are now a little less plentiful and therefore less cheap.

Fish. WHITE FISH. The same varieties are available as in April, except that you can now add plaice to the list. It is fat, without roe, and therefore an excellent buy. OILY FISH. This month sees the start of the herring season. Make full use of these excellent fish, which are cheap, nutritious, and just as good baked, grilled, fried, or soused, cold or hot. Because herrings are good so will be their products, bloaters and kippers. Another fish coming under this heading, and available from this month, is red mullet, which can be baked. SHELLFISH. Similar to April list, but oysters

[1] *See p 68.*

no longer in season and crayfish less good; you may be able to obtain crawfish instead.

Fruit. There will be plenty of cheap imported apricots at this time of the year. They are delicious stewed with cherries. The cherries on the market during this month are rarely English, but the Italian are excellent for cooking though not so good to eat as they lack the flavour and fleshiness of English fruit. First gooseberries available.

Meat. As for February (p 80), except that it is considered unwise to buy pork.

Vegetables. This may be called a luxury month for both fruit and vegetables. In addition to the green vegetables available in March we now see the first broad beans, asparagus, tiny marrows, and some of the early turnips and beetroot. First new English potatoes. Salad vegetables are more plentiful. English tomatoes while not cheap are more plentiful, lettuces, including cos lettuce, are good.

May Meals

MAY FIRST

Breakfast
Grapefruit[1]
Kippers
etc

Kippers

Allow one large or two small kippers per person. Cut off the heads, then wash and dry. Either cook under the grill, fry, or cook in hot water. The first methods will appeal to those who like their kippers crisp, the last to those who like them soft and rather underdone.

To Grill: Heat the grill, put the fish on the rack with a small knob of margarine on each fish. Cook rapidly for about 5 minutes. You need not turn the fish.

To Fry: Heat a little margarine in the frying-pan and fry the

[1] *See* p 70.

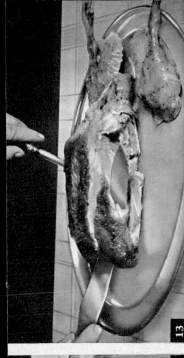

13

14

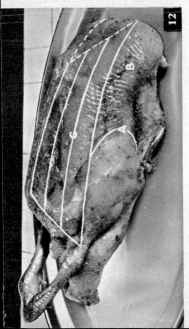

12

TO CARVE DUCK

The dotted lines in the picture above show the position of the wishbone. Remove leg and cut downwards in thick slices along lines C

Very small ducklings should be cut in two and each piece served complete with leg and breastbone (Page 35)

TO CARVE TURKEY

15. Cut off leg and carve as shown by A, B and C. This leaves body clear, and slices should be started high on one side of breast at D

16. Then bring knife down lower as at E (Page 35)

A FRUIT FLAN

17. Lining the flan tin. 18. To keep bottom of pastry case flat, cover with a piece of greaseproof paper carrying some haricot beans or a few crusts of bread. 19. Tinned fruit used in flans should be drained thoroughly. Do not fill case until it is cold (Page 126)

STEAK & KIDNEY PUDDING. Lining a basin with suet crust for steak and kidney pudding. The crust should be kept as flat as possible (Page 7

TOSSING A PANCAKE. How to hold the pan. The wrist should kept flexible and the pan jerked sharply upwards (Page 98)

fish on the underside first for about 3 minutes. Turn and cook for the same time.

With both grilling and frying serve on hot plates with any liquid left from cooking poured over.

In Hot Water: Stand the kippers in a large jug, then pour over boiling water. Leave for about 5 minutes. Drain, put onto hot plates, and put a knob of margarine on top. Or drain and put under a hot grill for one minute.

Main Meal of the Day (Lunch or Dinner)

Roast Lamb   Mint Sauce
New Potatoes   Broad Beans (with Parsley Sauce, if wished)[1]
Gooseberry Crumble

PLAN OF WORK

1. Make Mint Sauce.
2. Put meat into pre-heated oven.
3. Prepare vegetables.
4. Put gooseberries into oven, partly cook, prepare crumble pastry.
5. Put pastry on fruit. Return to oven.
6. Put on vegetables, after bringing water to boil.
7. Make gravy, and dish up first course.

Roast Lamb

Choose a suitable joint for roasting (as described on p 32). Put the meat into the roasting tin with about 2 oz dripping or lard. Keep the oven hot, Mark 6–7 or 425–450 deg. F., for the first 30 minutes of cooking time. After this the heat can be reduced to Mark 4–5 or 350–375 deg. F. (moderately hot).

Mint Sauce

2 heaped tablespoonfuls mint, chopped finely. 1 tablespoonful sugar, a little less may be preferred. 1 tablespoonful hot water. ½ teacup vinegar.

As you will see in the plan it is suggested the Mint Sauce is made some time before the meal. This allows the mint to infuse in the vinegar and you get a much better flavoured sauce. Put the

[1] *See* Vegetable table, p 38.

mint and sugar into a sauceboat, add the hot water, then pour on the vinegar, and allow to stand. The hot water brings out the flavour of the mint.

Broad Beans with Parsley Sauce

Cook the beans as in the Vegetable table (p 38), then either toss in melted margarine or put them into a vegetable dish and pour parsley sauce over. This is made by using the white sauce recipe (p 74) and adding about a tablespoonful finely chopped parsley.

Gooseberry Crumble

1 lb gooseberries. 1 good tablespoonful sugar or golden syrup to sweeten. Little water.

FOR THE CRUMBLE PASTRY. *4 oz flour (plain or self-raising). 3 oz margarine. 2 oz sugar.*

Put the fruit with the sugar and enough water to come halfway up the fruit, into a pie dish. Cook gently for about 15 minutes in a moderately hot oven, Mark 4–5 or 350–375 deg. F. Meanwhile prepare the pastry as follows: rub the margarine lightly into the flour, then stir in the sugar. Sprinkle this over the top of the hot fruit. Return to the oven for a further 30 minutes until the topping is crisp and brown.

To make any fruit crumble. If fruit is under-ripe or takes a fairly long time to cook, ie, apples, plums, damsons, etc, proceed as for gooseberries. For soft fruit or very ripe fruit, ie, raspberries, currants, etc, put the crumble on the cold fruit.

Light Lunch or Supper

Stuffed Eggs
Green, Potato, or Russian Salad[1]

Stuffed Eggs

Allow 1 hard-boiled egg for each person. Cut the eggs in halves carefully, then take out the yolk. Mash this and mix with a small knob of margarine or butter, salt, pepper, and either mashed sardines, little chopped ham, or grated cheese. Pile back into white cases and serve with green, potato, or Russian salad.

[1] *See p 96.*

MAY SECOND

Breakfast
Cereal
Poached Eggs
etc

Poached Eggs

Like all egg dishes poached eggs must be served the moment they are cooked, so it is advisable to toast the bread while they cook. Carefully crack the shells and pour the eggs into a cup or saucer so they do not break. Do not cook until water is boiling.

There are three ways of poaching eggs.

1. You may have a proper egg-poacher – with metal 'cups' over a rack. If using this put a piece of margarine, about the size of a hazel nut, into each cup, wait until this is melted, then carefully slide the egg into the cup, adding a pinch salt if wished. Put on the lid and allow the water in the pan underneath to boil steadily for about 3½–4 minutes. Slide the egg on to the buttered toast.

2. Put a small piece of margarine into an old cup, and stand it in a pan of boiling water to melt this. Pour in egg, put a lid on saucepan, and cook as before.

3. This method is preferred by many people since it gives a lighter result. Bring a good ½ pint of water to the boil in either a saucepan or frying-pan. Add a dessertspoonful vinegar, for this prevents the egg whites from spreading. Put in a good pinch salt. Slide the eggs into the boiling water, leave for about 3 minutes, or until egg white seems set. Insert spoon or fish slice, bring out the eggs carefully, and put on toast.

Main Meal of the Day (Lunch or Dinner)
Fried Plaice
Chipped Potatoes   Creamed Spinach
Bread and Butter Pudding

PLAN OF WORK

1. Prepare Bread and Butter Pudding.
2. Prepare vegetables.
3. Blanch potatoes.

4. Put on spinach.
5. Coat and fry fish – drain and keep hot.
6. Give potatoes final fry.
7. Dish up first course.

In most meals you will find I try not to use the oven more than necessary when cooking the main part of the meal on top of the cooker. In this case, however, it is wise to choose a pudding that requires cooking in a low oven, with little attention, for you will find the oven heat useful for keeping fish hot, while frying the potatoes the second time. Frying is the most difficult method of cooking to do well, so try to give as much time as possible to it the first time or so. After that you'll have little or no difficulty.

Fried Plaice and Chipped Potatoes

I give as an alternative the method of working with only one frying-pan, but, if you possibly can, have two pans, or one frying-pan and one deep fat pan, so that you can cook fish and chips separately. If cooking them in the same fat there is a tendency for the breadcrumbs from the fish to come off and spoil the clarity of the fat for the potatoes. This is less obvious when using a batter.

To Prepare Fish for Frying
(with egg and breadcrumb coating)

1. Wash the fish and dry it well.
2. Dust lightly with a little flour; this is important as it makes certain the fish is quite dry.
3. Beat an egg lightly with a fork in a flat dish, then brush the beaten egg over both sides of the fish.
4. Put about 3 tablespoonfuls crisp breadcrumbs in greaseproof paper, and toss the fish in this until well coated. Shake each piece of fish lightly to get rid of surplus crumbs, since these might burn in the fat.

Note. You will use this method whether using cutlets of fish, whole fish, or fillets. Plaice is generally fried whole or filleted; ask the fishmonger to fillet plaice. There is no need to remove the skin from the fish (or fillets) unless this is particularly disliked; again, a good fishmonger will do this for you. Cod is a difficult fish to fry, for it has large flakes and is therefore inclined to break easily. Coat twice with flour before dipping in egg and bread-crumbs or batter. Handle carefully.

To Prepare Fish for Frying
(with a batter coating)

1. Wash fish and dry it well.
2. Dust lightly with a little flour.
3. Make up batter (*see* below).
4. Pour batter into shallow dish, then lay the pieces of fish in this just before frying.

THE BATTER. *2 oz flour (plain or self-raising). Pinch salt. 1 egg. 4 tablespoonfuls ($\frac{1}{2}$ teacup) milk or milk and water. Beat flour, eggs, and salt until smooth, then gradually stir in the liquid.*

Use either a shallow frying-pan or a pan of deep fat. Fish can be fried quite satisfactorily in shallow fat, especially when coated with egg and breadcrumbs.

To Fry Fish in Shallow Fat. Put 3–4 oz lard or olive oil (this is an excellent frying medium) into the frying-pan. Heat *steadily* until you begin to see a faint haze when you look at the pan. Test by dropping in a small cube of bread, and when this turns a pale golden colour, in about 1 minute, the fat is ready. If by chance the bread turns colour more quickly, carefully take pan away from heat, or turn out gas, so that the fat cools slightly. Always be careful not to overheat fat, otherwise it burns before cooking the fish. When you are sure the fat is the right heat carefully lower the fish into it and cook steadily for several minutes in the case of whole fish or cutlets, then turn over and cook on the other side for the same length of time. When both sides are golden coloured, it is advisable to lower the heat for a few minutes to make sure the fish is cooked through to the middle. Fillets of plaice will need only about 2 minutes on either side.

To Fry Fish in Deep Fat. If you are fond of fried foods it is well worth while investing in a deep fryer with a frying basket (*see* p 13), for foods cooked in this way are much dryer, and the result much more professional in appearance. To begin with it does mean a lot of fat – at least 1 lb of lard or 1–1$\frac{1}{2}$ pints of oil to give any depth in a frying basket, but with care you can keep

117

this fat for some time. Also, the amount of fat absorbed by food fried in deep fat is much less than in shallow frying, so in the end it is more economical. After you have used the fat allow it to cool, then store (in the pan in which you have cooked the food if possible) in a cool place. Should you not be using the fat for several days in hot weather you *must* bring it to the boil; this is best done daily.

After using the fat once or twice it must be cleaned. Allow to become quite cold, cover with water, bring water and fat slowly to the boil, then allow to cool. Pour away the water, which will carry off any impurities.

When cooking fish in deep fat heat at least 1 lb lard or 1–1½ pints of oil *steadily* in the pan. Test as for shallow fat. Put in the basket (which will be used to remove the fish) but lower the fish in gently by hand. The reason for this is to prevent any possibility of the coated fish sticking to the basket and being difficult to take out. Cook as in shallow fat, but you will not need to turn fish. The moment the food goes into the pan, lower the heat, and *never overfill with either fat or food*, otherwise there is a danger of fat boiling over. Also too much food lowers the temperature of the fat and gives unsuccessful results. Remove the fish with the basket, hold for a minute over the fat to drain, then transfer (as in the case of shallow fat) onto crumpled tissue paper on a hot dish. This drains the last of the fat, so the fish is perfectly dry and crisp. Just before serving put the hot fish onto hot dish and garnish with lemon and parsley.

Fried Potatoes, or Chipped Potatoes

Peel potatoes, then cut into long fingers, as even in thickness as possible. Wash these, then dry well in a cloth and keep in a cloth until ready to cook, so that they are as dry as possible and there is no chance of their discolouring, as they will when left out in the air.

Frying Potatoes in Deep Fat. Heat and test the fat as described in method of cooking fish. If preferred, instead of using a cube of bread use one chip. When you think the fat is hot enough drop this in and watch carefully. If the potato sinks to the bottom, and there is no movement of the fat, then you must get it hotter. If, however, the fat bubbles immediately the chip is put in – and the chip stays at the top of the fat – then the fat is the right heat, at which temperature it is driving off the moisture from the potatoes. Put enough chips into the frying-basket to about one-quarter fill it. Lower carefully into the fat, watching to see there is no danger of it overflowing. This will not happen if you don't use more fat than will half fill the pan, and cook small quantities of food only at one time. Cook the potatoes for about 3 minutes; when you test one chip with the point of a knife it should feel soft. They will still be white. Remove the potatoes with the basket and stand on a plate. Just before serving the chips, re-heat the fat, test to make sure it is hot enough, and fry rapidly for about 2 minutes until crisp and brown. Drain on crumpled tissue paper.

Frying Potatoes in Shallow Fat. Follow the same method as for frying the fish, testing the fat to see if hot enough. Fry the potatoes, turning when brown on one side until crisp and golden brown. This method gives quite good chips, but there is no doubt that deep frying is better.

To Fry Fish and Potatoes in One Container. (1) Deep fat. Give the potatoes the first frying, remove, put in fish and cook. Drain and keep hot, then give final frying to potatoes. 2. Shallow fat. Fry fish first, drain and keep hot, then cook potatoes. If there appear to be a lot of breadcrumbs in the pan it is advisable to wash this after frying the fish, and before cooking the potatoes.

Creamed Spinach

Cook spinach as directed in Vegetable table (p 41), then drain carefully. Either rub through a sieve or turn onto your chopping board and chop until the vegetable is very fine. Heat 1 oz margarine and 2 tablespoonfuls cream together in a saucepan, then add the spinach and heat together gently.

Bread and Butter Pudding

3 slices of bread and butter, cut from a large loaf, but very thin. 2 tablespoonfuls dried fruit. 1 good tablespoonful sugar. 1 egg. ½ pint milk.

Divide the bread and butter into neat triangles, then arrange in a greased pie dish. Beat the egg, pour the warmed milk over it, add half the sugar and the dried fruit. Pour over the bread and butter, and dust the top with sugar. Cook for about 45 minutes in very moderate oven, Mark 3–4 or 325–350 deg. F., when the custard should be set. The last quarter of an hour move the dish to the top of the oven so that it browns and becomes crisp.

Light Lunch or Supper

Cheese Pudding
Jacket Potatoes[1]   *Baked Tomatoes*
Note. The potatoes must be put into the oven before the pudding.

Cheese Pudding

1 large egg or 2 small eggs. ½ pint milk. 2 oz grated cheese. 1½ teacups breadcrumbs.[2] *Good pinch salt, pepper, mustard. ½–1 oz margarine.*

Heat the milk, then stir in the crumbs, cheese, seasoning, and margarine. Cool slightly, then beat in the egg. Pour into greased dish and bake for 30 minutes in a moderate to moderately hot oven (centre), Mark 5–6 or 375–400 deg. F., until golden brown on top and firm.

Baked Tomatoes

Allow 1 large or 2 small tomatoes for each person. Put into a dish with a tiny piece of margarine, and a sprinkling of salt and pepper on each tomato. Bake for 15 minutes near the top of a moderately hot oven, Mark 5–6 or 375–400 deg. F.

MAY THIRD

Breakfast

Fruit Juice[3]
Omelet
etc

Omelet

Don't let anyone persuade you that omelets are difficult to make. Like all egg dishes they are quickly made, but *must* be eaten as soon as they are cooked. The most suitable omelet for breakfast is a plain one, without fillings. Allow 1½–2 eggs per person. Beat the eggs in a basin. Don't forget to break them separately into

[1] *See p 88.*   [2] *See p 55.*   [3] *See p 84.*

a cup, in case one should be bad, before transferring them to the basin. Add a good pinch salt and pepper, and for each 2 eggs a tablespoonful water. Put a small knob of butter into your smallest pan (*see* notes on frying-pans, etc, p 13). When hot pour in the eggs. Leave for about a minute over a high heat, when the bottom will have set, then loosen the egg mixture from the sides of the pan and cook rapidly, tipping the pan from side to side so that the liquid egg flows underneath and cooks quickly. When the egg is as set as you like it, for taste varies, slip your palette knife under the omelet and fold it away from the handle. Grasp the handle firmly and tip onto a hot plate or dish. Garnish with parsley. In the morning, when speed is important, you may prefer to cook one large omelet, but don't cook more than 4 eggs in a 6-inch pan, otherwise cooking takes too long and the omelet is tough. (Pls. 22, 23.)

Main Meal of the Day (Lunch or Dinner)

Beef Galantine

Salads

Rice Pudding   Stewed Apricots and Cherries

PLAN OF WORK

1. Make galantine as early as possible, so that it has time to cool. (It is a good idea to make this overnight.)
2. Put Rice Pudding in the oven.
3. Complete galantine.
4. Put fruit in oven.
5. Prepare salads, and dish up first course.

Beef Galantine

1 lb minced stewing beef. ½ lb sausage meat. 2 teacups breadcrumbs (see p 55). 1 egg. 1 pint stock, or, when not available, milk. Salt, pepper, mustard. Pinch dried mixed herbs.

Get the butcher to mince the meat, or put it through your own mincer. When buying ready-minced beef see that it has not become dry on the outside, and has not a high proportion of fat and gristle. Stir the minced beef into the sausage meat, then add all the other ingredients, mixing thoroughly with a fork. Either press the mixture into a well-greased basin, or form it into a roll and put into a piece of linen cloth. An old, but of course perfectly clean, and plain white, teacloth would do. Tie each end. If using a basin cover with greased greaseproof paper (*see* p 78). Steam the galantine for 2 hours. Turn out and cool. Cut into neat slices to serve.

Rice Pudding

2 oz rice. 1 oz sugar, or a little less, according to taste. 1 pint milk. 1 level tablespoonful suet or small knob of margarine.

Put the washed rice into a pie dish, pour over the milk, add sugar and suet or margarine. The fat is not essential, but it does make a more creamy pudding. Put into a very low oven, Mark 1–2 or 275–300 deg. F., and cook for about 2 hours. Long slow cooking is the secret of a creamy milk pudding.

Stewed Apricots and Cherries

½ lb cherries. ½ lb apricots. 2 oz sugar or golden syrup. Water.

Halve the apricots, and remove stones. Put these, together with the cherries, in a sieve or colander and wash under running water. Dry, then put into a pie dish with the sugar, and half cover with water. Put a piece of paper over the top of the fruit or a lid on the dish and cook for 45–50 minutes in a very low oven, Mark 1–2 or 275–300 deg. F.

HINTS ON STEWING FRUIT

This is one way of stewing fruit. You can also cook it in a saucepan, but remember the following points:

1. Don't use too much water. Some watery fruits, eg, rhubarb, raspberries, currants, need practically no water; others should be only half covered.
2. If you wish to keep the fruit a good shape always boil sugar and water together first, then drop in the fruit and simmer gently.
3. Always cook the fruit slowly, otherwise it breaks badly before being softened through to the middle.

Light Lunch or Supper

Soused Herrings
Tomato and Watercress Salad

122

Soused Herrings

4 large or 8 small herrings. 1 small onion. 1 teaspoonful pickling spice (bought by the ounce). 1 teaspoonful sugar. 1 teaspoonful allspice. 1 teacup water. 1 teacup vinegar. Good pinch pepper. ½ teaspoonful salt.

Wash the herrings. Cut off the heads, if the fishmonger has not done so. To remove the bones lay the fish on your chopping board and run your thumb very hard up and down the side, where you will feel the backbone. Split the fish down the stomach with a sharp knife. You will now have a flat fish. Insert the point of the knife under the bone or take the bone between finger and thumb and you will find that it comes away easily. Roll the herrings from the head end, then arrange the rolls with the tails standing jauntily upwards in a dish. Slice the onion, and add all the ingredients. Either put a piece of paper or a lid on the dish and cook very slowly in the oven, Mark 1–2 or 275–300 deg. F., for about 1 hour. Leave in the vinegar until cold.

Tomato and Watercress Salad

Arrange alternate layers of tomatoes and watercress in a dish until it is full, ending with watercress. Pour over a little of the vinegar from the soused herrings and add a good shake of salt and pepper.

June Shopping

At last we see the beginning of a profusion of English fruits. This is the month I would make gooseberry jam, and towards the very end of the month, if it has been a good hot season, strawberries are cheap and good, so make strawberry jam (*see* p 205 for instructions).

Gooseberries are an excellent fruit to bottle, but strawberries or cherries tend to lose their flavour when bottled. You could, however, add these fruits to a summer fruit salad to be bottled (*see* p 206).

FOODS IN SEASON

Be most careful about storing uncooked fish, meat, and all dairy products during the next months. Keep them in a *cool place, covered.* Put muslin moistened with vinegar round fish and meat, for the smell of vinegar is an excellent deterrent to flies.

Eggs are becoming less plentiful.

Fish. As for May, except that oysters will be out of season.

Fruit. The familiar apples and oranges are sometimes scarce during this month, but as compensation there will be cherries, gooseberries, and strawberries.

Meat. As for February, except that it is considered unwise to buy pork; otherwise most meats are plentiful and good.

Vegetables. Very much as May except that young vegetables, such as broad beans, garden peas, asparagus, new turnips, are much cheaper. If you are fond of broad beans have them this month, for after June the outside gets very tough, and they are hardly worth cooking.

June Meals

During the next three months it is assumed that most people would rather have a cereal or fresh fruit with toast than a cooked breakfast, so breakfast dishes have not been given. If you feel cooked breakfasts are essential for your family, have lean bacon, eggs, cold ham, tongue. Avoid very fat foods during hot weather.

JUNE FIRST

Main Meal of the Day (Lunch or Dinner)
Braised Rib of Beef
New Potatoes[1]   *Broad Beans*[1]   *New Carrots*[1]
Cherry Flan

PLAN OF WORK
1. Prepare vegetables.
2. Commence cooking braised beef.
3. Cook flan and cool.
4. Simmer cherries in syrup, strain and cool.
5. Complete flan.
6. Put on water for vegetables.
7. Cook vegetables.
8. Dish up first course.

[1] *See* Vegetable table, pp 38, 39, 40.

Braised Beef

Piece of rib of beef, about 2 lb. 2 oz dripping or lard. 2 oz flour. 1½ pints water or stock. 2 onions. 3 carrots (if small use about 6 carrots). Salt, pepper, mustard.

Heat the dripping in a saucepan, then put in the beef and cook steadily for about 5 minutes on either side. Lift out into deep casserole, then fry the sliced onions and carrots in the remaining fat for about 4 minutes. Lift these into casserole also. Blend the flour carefully with the fat, and cook over a steady heat until it goes dark brown, but be careful not to let it burn. Remove from the heat, and gradually stir in the water or stock. Return to the heat and bring to the boil, cooking until thickened. Season well. Pour over the beef. Put the lid on the casserole and cook in a very slow oven, Mark 1–2 or 275–300 deg. F., for about 2½ hours. Serve on hot dish garnished with the vegetables, and some of the freshly cooked new carrots. The carrots and broad beans can be cooked together.

Cherry Flan

1 7-inch flan ring, made of short-crust pastry. 1 lb cherries. ¼ pint water. 2 oz sugar. ½ teaspoonful arrowroot or cornflour.

First make and bake the flan case (as directions given for Lemon Meringue Pie, p 65). Allow it to cool. Put the sugar and water in a saucepan and boil together until the sugar has melted. Put in the cherries and allow to stand in the syrup, with no heat underneath, for about 10 minutes. Drain through a sieve. If by chance the cherries are under-ripe they must be simmered in the syrup for about 5 minutes. Let the cherries become quite cold. Pack the cherries into the flan case. Blend the teaspoonful arrowroot with ½ teacup of the syrup, stirring until smooth. Add to the rest of the syrup in the saucepan, and cook, stirring all the time, until thick and clear. Cool slightly, then carefully pour over the fruit in the flan ring.

Variations

Most dessert fruits are delicious in a flan case, but in order to keep the pastry crisp, do *not* put in the fruit or syrup until the pastry has cooled, the fruit is cold, and the syrup nearly cold. *Soft fruits*, such as raspberries and strawberries, should be put into the hot syrup and left there until cold. *Tinned fruits*, such as

125

peaches, need not be heated, but drain carefully, and thicken the syrup from the tin. (Pls. 17, 18, 19.)

Light Lunch or Supper

Prawn Mayonnaise. *For 4 people allow about 1½ pints prawns.* Prepare the prawns (which you buy already cooked) by removing the heads and the brittle shells and legs.

Pile the prepared fish in the centre of the plates, and arrange an attractive salad round (p 68). Pour mayonnaise on the fish. Serve also with potato salad (p 67) if wished.

JUNE SECOND

Main Meal of the Day (Lunch or Dinner)
Cornish Pasties
Salad[1]   New Potatoes
Egg Custard   Fruit Salad

PLAN OF WORK

1. Make and cook the Cornish Pasties if you want them cold for the meal.
2. Prepare the Fruit Salad.
3. Cook Egg Custard, cooling oven if it is to be baked.
4. Prepare potatoes, then after the water is boiling cook these.
5. Make the Salad.
6. Dish up first course.

Cornish Pasties

THE PASTRY. *8 oz flour. 4 oz fat (2 oz margarine, 2 oz lard). Good pinch salt. Water to mix.*

THE FILLING. *4–6 oz uncooked rump steak or good quality stewing steak. 2 medium-sized potatoes or equivalent in small potatoes. 1 large onion. ½ teacup stock or gravy (or water flavoured with a little Marmite). Salt, pepper, mustard. Egg or milk to glaze.*

First make the pastry (*see* p 156). Roll this out to about ¼ inch thick, then cut into 4 rounds about the size of a large tea plate. Cut the meat into tiny pieces, then dice the potatoes and onion. Mix these together, adding seasoning. Put a good pile in the centre of each round, and moisten with a little of the stock.

[1] *See* recipes for salads, pp 67, 68.

126

Brush the edges of the pastry with water, then bring these together in the centre (*see* Pl. 24). Press them tightly, so that there is no possibility of their opening during cooking, and stand the pasties on a baking tray. Brush the outside with either a little milk or beaten egg to give a slight glaze. Any egg left on this occasion can be put in custard.

Note. When using part of an egg for glazing, pour a little cold water over the remainder, so that it can be used on a further occasion. If you leave it without water a thick skin develops on top.

Stand the pasties in the centre of a hot oven, Mark 6–7 or 425–450 deg. F., and bake for about 25 minutes. Lower the heat to moderate, Mark 4–5 or 350–375 deg. F., for a further 35 minutes to make sure the meat is cooked inside.

CORNISH PASTIES WITH COOKED MEAT

The pasties can be made with left-over cooked meat, in which case they will take only about 25 minutes in a hot oven, and a further 5 minutes in a moderate heat (to make sure the meat is hot and the vegetables cooked). In this case the potatoes and onions *must* be diced finely or grated.

Egg Custard
(steamed or baked)

2 eggs. 1 level tablespoonful sugar. ¾ pint milk. Little grated nutmeg.

Beat the eggs with a fork, add the sugar, and the warmed milk. The milk *must not boil* otherwise it will curdle the eggs. Pour into a greased pie dish or basin, grating the nutmeg on top.

Baked Custard. Half-fill a dish, slightly larger than the pie dish, with cold water. Stand the pie dish in this and bake for about 1¼ hours in the centre of a very moderate oven, Mark 1–2 or 275–300 deg. F., until firm. Too great a heat causes curdling, and this spoils the custard.

Steamed Custard. Put the basin into the steamer over very hot water and cook steadily for about 1¼ hours. The water must never boil, otherwise the custard will curdle. Test with your finger; if you can just bear it in the water, the heat is right.

Cool slightly, then you can turn out the custard, if wished.

Fruit Salad

About 1 lb mixed dessert fruit, cherries, strawberries, orange, apple. 1½ teacups water. Squeeze of lemon juice. 2 oz sugar.

A perfect fruit salad is one in which the fruit is whole, and fresh-flavoured. Put the fruit into a bowl. Boil together sugar, water, and lemon juice, until the sugar has dissolved, then cool slightly, so that it will not crack the bowl. Pour over the fruit, and leave until cold.

Light Lunch or Supper

Grilled Mackerel
Gooseberry Sauce or Parsley Butter (Maître d'Hôtel Butter)

Grilled Mackerel

4 mackerel. 1 oz margarine. Salt, pepper. Lemon. Parsley.

Cut the heads off the mackerel, and remove bones (*see* method used for herrings, p 123). Heat the grill. Fold the mackerel over again after you have taken out the bones. Put the fish on the grill grid, with a small knob of margarine on each, and sprinkle with salt and pepper. Cook rapidly for about 4 minutes, turn the fish, put a little more margarine on top and seasoning, and cook for a further 4 minutes. Lower the heat of the grill to give a further 2 or 3 minutes cooking. These are solid fish, and therefore take rather a long time to cook. Serve on hot dish, with any margarine that has dropped into the grill pan poured over. Garnish with rings of lemon and sprigs of parsley.

Gooseberry Sauce

½ lb gooseberries. ¾ teacup water. 1 or 2 tablespoonfuls sugar. ½ oz margarine.

Remove the tiny stalks from the fruit, and the flower buds. This is called 'topping and tailing'. Put into a saucepan with the water, sugar, and margarine. Simmer slowly until a very smooth mixture, then either rub through a sieve or beat with a wooden spoon until smooth. This fruit sauce is delicious with mackerel.

Parsley Butter

1 oz butter or margarine. 1 teaspoonful lemon juice. Salt, pepper. 1 tablespoonful chopped parsley.

Cream the margarine with the lemon juice, and seasoning. Add parsley. When parsley has been mixed in, leave in a cold place. Put a small knob of this on each fish before bringing to the table.

JUNE THIRD

Main Meal of the Day (Lunch or Dinner)

Calf's Head   Brain Sauce
Peas[1]   New Potatoes[1]
Strawberry Shortcake

PLAN OF WORK

1. Prepare Calf's Head, and put on to cook.
2. Make and cook Shortcake.
3. Prepare vegetables.
4. When cool fill shortcake with fruit.
5. Put on water for potatoes, then cook these.
6. Put on water for peas, then cook these.
7. Cut meat from bones of Calf's Head, then make the sauce.
8. Dish up Calf's Head and vegetables.

Calf's Head

1 calf's head (half is enough for a meal for 4 people, but the other half can be cooked for brawn).[2] 2 carrots. 2 onions. Water, salt, pepper. ½ pint white sauce (see p 74).

Have the calf's head cut in halves by the butcher. Put both halves into a large saucepan, with the vegetables and seasoning, then just cover with cold water. Simmer gently for 2½–3 hours. Lift out one half of the head, cut the meat from the bones, and put this onto a hot dish. Take out the brains (soft white part of the head) and stir into the white sauce. Serve this sauce over the meat, garnished with the vegetables from the stock, and a few of the freshly cooked vegetables.

Strawberry Shortcake

4 oz margarine. 4 oz sugar. 1 egg. 6 oz flour (with plain flour use 1½ teaspoonfuls baking powder). Little lard and flour for greasing tins. ¾–1 lb strawberries. Sugar for dusting. Cream.

[1] *See Vegetable table, p 40.*   [2] *See p 130.*

Cream together the margarine and sugar, then beat in the egg. Lastly stir in the flour. Grease 2 6-inch sandwich tins with a little lard. To do this either melt about ½ oz lard in a pan (or jar standing in hot water), then brush over the tins with your pastry brush, or put the lard onto a piece of greaseproof paper and rub over the tins. The first method is considered better, for it gives a more even coating. Shake on a little flour, so that you have a fine coating all over the tins. Tap these sharply on the table to get rid of the surplus flour. Divide the shortcake mixture into halves, and spread or press each half in the tins. The mixture will be firm enough to handle, but rather too sticky to roll. Bake for 15 minutes near the top of a moderate to moderately hot oven, Mark 5–6 or 375–400 deg. F. Turn out and cool on a wire sieve. When cold, sandwich together with a thick layer of sliced strawberries, dusted with sugar, and spread with whipped cream, if wished. Put on the other shortcake, and stand the rest of the strawberries on top. Decorate again with whipped cream.

To Whip Cream. Put the cream into a perfectly dry basin, whip sharply with an egg whisk until stiff, then stir in a little sugar. Don't over-whip, otherwise it has a 'buttery' taste.

To Make a Mock Cream. Cream together 2 oz margarine or butter with 2 oz castor sugar, until they are very soft and white. *Gradually* beat in 2 tablespoonfuls hot water. This cream has an excellent flavour, especially when using butter, and is as thick as whipped cream.

Light Lunch or Supper

Calf's Head Brawn

To make this cut all the meat from the second half of the head (the first being used for a hot meal). Put this into a basin. Boil the stock until only about ¼ of a pint remains, taste to make sure it wants no more seasoning, then strain over the meat. Leave in a cold place until set.

This is a delicious cold dish. If you buy half a head to make brawn only, then it should be cooked as directions on p 129.

July Shopping

In July there should be unlimited salads, and fruit will be good and plentiful. This is the month to make redcurrant jelly and blackcurrant jam and, towards the end of the month, raspberry jam. Directions for these jams are in Section IV.

All these fruits are excellent when bottled, though redcurrants are better mixed with other fruit, for they contain so many pips. You will find the more exotic vegetables included in the lists this month. Try them, for they can make a complete dish in themselves.

If the weather is very hot do use every care in storing foods.

To Store Foods in Hot Weather

Butter and Cooking Fats. Put in earthenware dishes and stand these in another dish of cold water. Cover with muslin and allow the ends to stand in the cold water. A good tablespoonful salt added to the water helps to keep temperature low.

Fruit. The skins of fruit should be well washed before eating them, and particular care paid to this in hot weather, when flies are so troublesome. Soft fruits should be removed from their bags or punnets and put on to large dishes so that they are kept as cool as possible.

Milk. If your storage cupboards are warm, then undoubtedly you will be well advised to put the milk into saucepans, bringing it *almost* to boiling point. Don't allow the milk to boil for any length of time. You can let the milk cool, then store in wide-topped jugs, covered with damp muslin. If the weather is only moderately hot you can just stand the milk bottles, etc, in cold water, or if you have vacuum flasks at home pour the milk into these the moment it arrives. A vacuum flask not only keeps food hot, it keeps it cold just as efficiently. As pointed out under June (p 123) great care should be taken to store fish and meat. Many people prefer to cook their joints the moment they arrive from the butcher. Even so, be careful how you store cooked meat, fish, etc. Keep the food cool – and keep it covered.

Vegetables. Green vegetables and salads 'wilt' very quickly in hot sun. When you get the vegetables home remove them from the basket as soon as possible, for they generate heat and so become spoiled quickly. Lay green vegetables out flat in a cool place, the concrete floor of an airy shed is ideal. If you have to

131

store them overnight sprinkle with water. If you have an airy vegetable rack put this in the coolest place possible. Peas and beans also keep better if spread out flat. Salads will, of course, be put into the refrigerator (*see* p 28) if you are fortunate enough to have one. Failing this you can either spread out as suggested for vegetables or put lettuce, parsley, and watercress in an airtight biscuit tin overnight.

FOODS IN SEASON

Eggs. Less plentiful, but should be enough without using preserved.

Fish. Exactly the same fish available as in April, May, and June. Shellfish like prawns, etc, make delicious salads, but make sure you buy them from a shop which has a reputation for fresh fish.

Fruit. There will still be cherries, gooseberries, strawberries, and plentiful supplies of loganberries, red and black-currants, and raspberries. Melons also should be available. Good quality oranges, apples, and pears may be difficult to get.

Meat. As in May and June it is unwise to cook pork this month, and be particularly careful that sausages are bought fresh and cooked and eaten quickly. Other meats should be good, but wash in plenty of cold water and vinegar before cooking – 1 tablespoonful vinegar to 1 pint water.

Vegetables. GREEN VEGETABLES. Cabbage, cabbage greens, cauliflower, spinach are the best of the green vegetables. Also in season are asparagus, broad beans (though getting older), french beans, marrows (still young and small). ROOT VEGETABLES. All the new season's young vegetables – beetroot, carrots, swedes, turnips – should be available, and when small and young have excellent flavour.

The *imported vegetables* include aubergines (egg plant), capsicums (or green and red peppers); not the same as the tiny red peppers that are used for adding flavouring to soups and stews. *To Cook Aubergines.* Split down the centre, remove the pulp, and mix this with minced meat, breadcrumbs, and an egg. Pile back again, and bake for about 45 minutes in a moderately hot oven.

132

To Cook Green Peppers. Split and stuff in the same way as aubergines, and bake for 45 minutes. Slice finely and mix in salads, or slice and fry gently. Large red peppers or capsicums can be used in the same way.

July Meals

JULY FIRST

Main Meal of the Day (Lunch or Dinner)

Baked Stuffed Hearts
French Beans[1]   *New Potatoes (Boiled or Roasted)*[1]
Raspberry Summer Pudding

PLAN OF WORK

1. Make the Summer Pudding, so it has some hours to stand (preferably overnight).
2. Prepare the stuffing for the hearts, then after pre-heating the oven, cook these.
3. Put on water for vegetables, then cook them.
4. Turn out Summer Pudding.
5. Make gravy, then serve first course.

Baked Stuffed Hearts

2–3 sheep's hearts. 2–3 oz dripping, or lard. Sage and Onion stuffing (see p 64).

Put the hearts into cold water with a teaspoonful salt for about 20 minutes. This draws out the blood. Dry the hearts well, then fill with the stuffing. If you find it difficult to get the stuffing into the centre of the hearts, cut them in halves and spread the stuffing between the two halves, then put together and tie firmly with cotton. Put into roasting tin with the dripping, and cook in a moderate to moderately hot oven, Mark 5–6 or 375–400 deg. F., for about 60 minutes. To serve cut into slices.

Roast New Potatoes

These have a delicious flavour. They take about 45 minutes in hot fat in a moderately hot oven. Allow fat to get very hot round

[1] *See* Vegetable table, pp 38, 40.

133

the hearts, dry potatoes carefully, dust with salt, then roll in the hot fat.

Raspberry Summer Pudding

About ½ a small loaf. 1 lb raspberries. ½ teacup water. 2 oz sugar.

Cut the loaf into thin slices, removing the crusts if you wish. Line a pint basin with the bread, making sure every part of the basin is covered. Heat the water and sugar, put in the raspberries, and just heat through; do not overcook. Pour the raspberry mixture into the bread-lined basin. Cover with another thin layer of bread. Put a saucer on top of the pudding, with a weight of some kind, and leave until quite cold. Turn out carefully, and serve with cream from the top of the milk or cold custard sauce. This is a very surprising pudding, for the fruit soaks into the bread and no one would think that only bread had formed the 'crust'.

Variations

A mixture of raspberries and red and black currants. Plums when in season.

Light Lunch or Supper

Scotch Eggs
Salads

Scotch Eggs

1 lb sausage meat. 4 hard-boiled eggs. Little flour.

For coating: *1 egg. 2 tablespoonfuls crisp breadcrumbs.*

For frying: *Either deep fat[1] or 2 oz lard or dripping.*

Divide the sausage meat into four parts. Lightly dust the pastry board with flour and roll out each 4 oz sausage meat to a neat square. Remove the shells from the hard-boiled eggs – you will find this easier to do if you plunge the eggs into cold water immediately after cooking them. Cooling quickly prevents a dark ring forming round the egg yolks. Put a hard-boiled egg on each square of sausage meat, then roll this round the egg until it is completely covered. Form the sausage meat into a neat shape, then brush with the beaten egg using a pastry brush. (*See* Pl. 25.)

[1] *See* p 117.

Put the breadcrumbs into greaseproof paper and toss the Scotch eggs in this until uniformly covered. Heat the fat until a very faint haze is seen; then put in the four sausage shapes. Cook steadily until golden brown. Drain, first on a fish slice, then on crumpled tissue paper. When cold and ready to serve cut into halves. Garnish with lettuce and sliced tomatoes.

JULY SECOND

Main Meal of the Day (Lunch or Dinner)

Fish Salad
New Potato Salad   French Bean Salad
Trifle

PLAN OF WORK

1. Cook fish, allow to cool, then prepare trifle.
2. Cook potatoes, and make potato salad.
3. Make fish and bean salads.
4. Decorate trifle.
5. Dish up first course.

Fish Salad

1–1¼ lb white fish, the most suitable for a salad being cod, hake, halibut, skate (particularly good), turbot or fresh haddock. Flat fish such as plaice and whiting are rather unsuitable, for they do not flake easily. ¼ pint mayonnaise. ½ teacup chopped cucumber. 1 tablespoonful vinegar or lemon juice. ½ or 2 hard-boiled eggs. Salt, pepper. For special occasions, few shrimps or prawns to garnish.

First cook the fish. To do this put into a steamer, adding a good sprinkling of salt and pepper, and cook over a pan of boiling water until the fish comes away from the bone and seems quite soft. The time required varies according to the thickness of the fish, but test after about 10 minutes. (If you do not possess a steamer then cook in about ½ pint water, with seasoning.) Drain the fish, remove skin and bones, then flake coarsely. When cold mix with the mayonnaise, cucumber (which should soak for about ¼ hour in the lemon juice or vinegar) and the chopped egg white. Pile on a bed of lettuce, and decorate with the chopped egg yolk.

New Potato Salad

Approximately 1 lb new potatoes.[1] 4–8 tablespoonfuls mayonnaise.[2] 1 tablespoonful finely chopped mint. 2 tablespoonfuls chopped apple. 1 tablespoonful chopped spring onion. Salt, pepper, paprika pepper.

Drain the potatoes and cut into halves (unless very small) while still hot. Mix with all the other ingredients, putting in approximately half the mayonnaise. I have given a variable quantity of mayonnaise, for some people prefer their salads rather drier than others. Pile into a dish, cover with the rest of the mayonnaise and paprika pepper.

French Bean Salad

Left-over French beans make a delicious salad. Simply toss them in a little French dressing.[3]

Trifle

3 sponge cakes. 1 good tablespoonful jam, preferably raspberry. 1 tablespoonful blanched almonds.[4] About ½ teacup fruit syrup, from a tin of fruit or from stewed fruit. 1 pint custard sauce, made according to directions on packet.

Split the sponge cakes into two or three layers and spread with jam. Put into a glass dish, and pour the fruit syrup over it, allowing it to soak into the sponge cakes. Pour the hot custard over. Put a plate on top to prevent a skin forming, and when cold decorate with the almonds.

Variations

Richer Trifle. Soak the sponge cakes with sherry instead of fruit syrup. Decorate the top with glacé cherries, whipped cream, angelica.

Fruit Trifle. Soak the sponge cakes with fruit syrup, but also put on a layer of tinned fruit, or fresh fruit soaked in hot syrup first. Decorate the top with whipped cream, whole fruit, and nuts.

Jelly Trifle. Make a pint of fruit-flavoured jelly. Soak the sponge cakes in a small quantity of fruit syrup, rather under ½ teacup,

[1] *See* Vegetable table, p 40. [2] *See* p 69.
 See p 69. [4] *See* p 48, Blanching.

otherwise the jelly will not set. Pour over half the hot jelly, together with fruit, if wished. Allow jelly to set, then pour cold custard over it. It must be cold, otherwise it will make the jelly soft again. When the custard is firm decorate with whipped jelly, cherries, nuts, and cream. To whip the jelly, put into a large bowl and whisk vigorously.

Light Lunch or Supper

Beef Rissoles
Fried Tomatoes[1]   *Sauté Potatoes*[2]

Beef Rissoles

8 oz cooked minced beef (or any left-over cooked meat). 1 grated large onion. ½ teaspoonful powdered sage. Rest of the ingredients as for Durham cutlets (see p 79).

Form the mixture into round flat cakes, and coat as for Durham cutlets. Fry in exactly the same way, and garnish each rissole with a slice of fried tomato. You could use uncooked meat, in which case it must be finely minced and the rissoles cooked a little longer and a little more slowly.

JULY THIRD

Main Meal of the Day (Lunch or Dinner)

Stewed Neck of Lamb, or Irish Stew
Young Carrots and Peas[3]
Blackcurrant Pudding

PLAN OF WORK

1. Prepare all vegetables.
2. Commence cooking Irish Stew.
3. Make Blackcurrant Pudding and put on to cook.
4. Add rest of potatoes to stew.
5. Put on water for carrots and peas, then cook these.
6. Dish up first course.

[1] *See* p 80.
[2] *See* p 83.
[3] *See* Vegetable table, pp 39, 40, but cook these together, adding pinch sugar and mint as for peas.

137

Stewed Neck of Lamb or Irish Stew

¾ lb neck of lamb. ½ lb onions. 1 lb potatoes. Salt, pepper.

First wash the meat and cut it into neat pieces. If using new potatoes cut one or two in halves, or if using old potatoes cut one large one into small slices. Slice the onions. Put the meat, pieces of potato and the sliced onions into the pan, adding about ¾ pint water and plenty of salt and pepper. Bring slowly to the boil, remove any scum, lower the heat, and simmer gently for just over 1½ hours. Add the rest of the potatoes, with a little more salt, and continue cooking for about 40 minutes. To serve, pile the meat and stock in the centre of the hot dish with the potatoes round and a garnish of the freshly cooked peas and carrots.

Blackcurrant Pudding

Suet Crust, as in Steak and Kidney Pudding (p 71). 1 lb black-currants. Water. 2 oz sugar or golden syrup.

Wash the blackcurrants, and remove any stalks. Make the suet pastry and line the basin as instructed on p 71. Put in the fruit, enough water to come halfway up, and sugar to taste – approximately 2 oz will be needed. Cover with the pastry and paper (again as instructed on p 71) and cook in the same way as Steak and Kidney Pudding for about 2 hours. Turn out and serve with custard sauce or cream.

Variations

This is a delicious boiled pudding, probably the richest of all fruit puddings, but you will find most fruits are excellent cooked in this way; try apples, plums, rhubarb, blackberries and apples, damsons, as each comes into season.

Light Lunch or Supper

Cheese Omelet
Tomato Purée

Cheese Omelet

Follow directions for making the omelet on p 120, but if possible make individual ones. Add the grated cheese just before folding the omelet, allowing 1 good tablespoonful cheese for each person. Put omelet onto hot dish and pour fresh tomato purée over it.

Tomato Purée

4 large tomatoes. 1 rasher of bacon. 1 small onion. ½ oz margarine.
Good pinch salt, pepper, sugar.

Heat the margarine in the bottom of a small saucepan, then fry
the very finely chopped (or grated) onion until soft. Add finely
chopped bacon (after removing the rind) and fry for several
minutes. Try not to allow either bacon or onion to become too
brown – which means a low heat and frequent stirring.

Cut the tomatoes into halves or quarters, add these to the
onion mixture, with a good pinch salt, pepper, and sugar. Simmer
gently until the mixture is very soft. Rub through a sieve if
wished or beat well with a wooden spoon. Taste the purée to
make sure you have added enough seasoning.

August Shopping

As August is so often a holiday month for a family with children
it is an excellent idea to plan as many cold dishes or picnic meals
as possible, so that everyone can enjoy the holiday period and –
we hope – the fine weather. You will find it rather an 'in between'
month for fruits; the soft fruits are getting scarce and therefore
expensive, and the plum crop is hardly ready. In the same way
vegetables tend to be a little difficult this month, for peas are
getting rather older and runner beans barely coming into season.

FOODS IN SEASON

Eggs may be less plentiful, but try not to use preserved eggs yet,
for during the late autumn months eggs are inclined to become
dearer, and you will be glad of your preserved eggs then.

Fish. WHITE FISH. Although there will be a reasonable selection,
cod and haddock are not at their best from now until October,
so try not to buy these. Plaice, sole, halibut, hake, turbot are all
very good. OILY FISH. Herrings still good, so are mackerel. This
is normally the last month that whitebait are really good, so if
you are fond of them make full use of these tiny, delicious fish.
There are both red and grey mullet, and fresh salmon is generally
at its cheapest in August. SHELLFISH. Crab, crawfish, lobster,
shrimps.

Fruit. While there may still be raspberries available, the early plums, small but of excellent flavour, are coming on the market. There will be some English apples, though the good cooking apples are not yet mature.

Meat. As for July.

Vegetables. Very much the same vegetables and salads available as in July, but look out for corn on the cob, and the first runner beans, though as yet they will be few and dear.

August Meals
AUGUST FIRST

Main Meal of the Day (Lunch or Dinner)
Roast Chicken with Veal Stuffing
Sausages   Bread Sauce
Roast New Potatoes in their Jackets   Sweetcorn or Peas[1]
Apple Charlotte

PLAN OF WORK

1. Prepare breadcrumbs for Bread Sauce; stuffing; Apple Charlotte.
2. Prepare vegetables.
3. Make Bread Sauce, so that it has plenty of time to infuse.
4. Make stuffing. Simmer giblets to give stock for gravy.
5. Prepare Apple Charlotte.
6. Stuff chicken and put into oven, which has been pre-heated.
7. Add potatoes and sausages round the roasting fowl.
8. Put Apple Charlotte into oven.
9. Bring water to boil for vegetables and cook this.
10. Allow Bread Sauce to heat through.
11. Make gravy, and dish up first course.

Bread Sauce

1 teacup breadcrumbs. 1–2 oz margarine. 1 small onion. ½ pint milk. 2 or 3 cloves, if liked. Salt, pepper.

Peel the onion, and if you are using cloves stick these firmly into the onion. Put this into the milk together with the other in-

[1] *See* Vegetable table, p 40.

140

gredients. Slowly bring the milk to the boil. Remove from the heat and stand in a warm place for as long as possible. As you will see in the Plan of Work, this is the first job – after preparing breadcrumbs, for if you don't let the mixture infuse the bread sauce is sadly lacking in flavour. Just before the meal is ready, heat the sauce gently, beating it well with a wooden spoon. Remove onion before putting into sauce boat.

Veal (Parsley and Herb) Stuffing

2 teacups of breadcrumbs (see p 55). 1 egg. 2 oz suet or melted margarine (the suet to be finely shredded – unless using packet suet). Seasoning. 2–3 teaspoonfuls chopped parsley. ½ teaspoonful mixed herbs. Grated rind and juice of ½ lemon.

Mix all the ingredients thoroughly together. The cooked meat from the giblets can be added to make a rich 'meaty' stuffing, if wished.

Roast Chicken

It is assumed that the chicken has been drawn and trussed, and is therefore all ready for the oven, for that is hardly a job for the beginner. Wash the bird under running cold water, and dry thoroughly. Lift the large flap of skin at the neck end, and press the stuffing in firmly. If you don't feel it is securely 'tucked in', then put a small sharp skewer through the bottom of the skin flap into the bird. You will often have skewers sent you from the butcher in a joint of meat, so save these, for they often come in useful. Don't forget to simmer giblets to make gravy. Put some rashers of fat bacon (the cheapest kind can be used, and often a grocer will sell you suitable fat pieces, if you explain you want it for basting a chicken) over the breast of the bird, for that is the part that is inclined to dry during cooking. If you do not use bacon, smear the breast and legs well with lard or dripping and put about 2–4 oz dripping in the baking tin. Cook for the first 30 minutes in a hot oven, Mark 6–7 or 425–450 deg. F., then lower the heat to moderately hot for the rest of the time. Baste once or twice during cooking (*see* p 48).

Roast Sausages

Prick the sausages and put round the bird about 45 minutes before it has finished cooking.

Roast New Potatoes in their Jackets

Scrub the potatoes, but don't scrape them and remove skin. This becomes crisp and you retain all the flavour of the potato. Put in the hot fat, turn round in this, so that whole potato becomes coated, and allow about 45 minutes cooking time.

Apple Charlotte

2 teacups breadcrumbs. 1 lb apples, peeled and cored. 3 oz sugar. 3 oz margarine. Juice and grated rind of a lemon.

Slice the apples thinly, and put into a saucepan with the lemon rind and juice and half the sugar. Simmer gently until softened slightly. Try not to add water, but if you don't, you must stir to prevent the fruit from sticking. Heat the margarine in a frying-pan and stir the crumbs in this until they are all coated with the margarine. Stir in the rest of the sugar. Put a layer of the crumb mixture in a pie dish, then a layer of apple, more crumbs, more apple, and a final layer of crumbs. Bake for about 45 minutes in a moderate to moderately hot oven, Mark 5–6 or 375–400 deg. F. Serve with cream or the top of the milk.

Light Lunch or Supper

Stuffed Tomato Salad
Potato Salad[1]

Stuffed Tomato Salad

4 very large tomatoes. 2 hard-boiled eggs. 2 oz grated cheese. 2 tablespoonfuls mayonnaise.[2] Salt, pepper. Lettuce, cooked peas, sliced cucumber.

Cut the tops off the tomatoes, and scoop out the centre pulp with a teaspoon. Put the pulp into a basin, chop it finely with a sharp knife, then mix with salt, pepper, chopped hard-boiled egg white, and cheese. If you like salads well seasoned shake a very little salt and pepper inside the tomato cases. Pile the egg and cheese filling into each tomato case. Arrange prepared lettuce (*see* p 74) on a flat dish, then a ring of cooked peas, then sliced cucumber (this can be left in a little seasoned vinegar for half an hour before using). Stand the tomatoes in the centre. Pour the mayonnaise over the top of each tomato and sprinkle over the chopped hard-boiled egg yolk.

[1] *See* p 67.   [2] *See* p 69.

AUGUST SECOND

Main Meal of the Day (Lunch or Dinner)

Grilled Cutlets, or Chops, and Tomatoes
Sauté New Potatoes[1]   Runner Beans[2]
Plum Custard Mould

PLAN OF WORK

1. Make the Plum Custard Mould.
2. Prepare vegetables.
3. Put on water for beans and commence to cook these.
4. Heat grill for a few minutes, then cook cutlets and tomatoes.
5. While meat, etc, is cooking fry Sauté Potatoes.
6. Dish up first course.

Grilled Cutlets and Tomatoes

Choose good lean mutton cutlets, or chops from loin of lamb
or pork. Allow one good-sized cutlet for each person. Trim off
any surplus fat, but leave some fat on to give flavour and help
keep the meat moist. Cut the tomatoes into halves – allow two
halves at least for each person. Put the tomatoes into the grill
pan, sprinkling a little salt and pepper on top, and then put the
grid over. Arrange the cutlets on this. When the grill is very hot
cook the chops quickly for about 4–5 minutes, then turn over and
cook for the same time on the second side. Both sides will now
be brown. If you like meat well done (and with pork this is essential) lower the grill and cook more slowly for a further 3–6
minutes. The time depends on the thickness of the meat. Put onto
a hot dish, surrounded by the tomatoes, and garnished with
parsley.
Note. If preferred you can fry the cutlets, and in this case you
can remove the bones and coat the cutlets with egg and breadcrumbs (as for Durham cutlets, p 79), then fry for about 10–12
minutes, turning after the one side is brown and lowering the
heat to cook gently through to the middle.

Plum Custard Mould

*1 lb plums. ½ teacup water. 3 oz sugar (or little less if the fruit is
very ripe). 2 level dessertspoonfuls custard powder. ½ pint milk.
1 teaspoonful powdered gelatine. 2 tablespoonfuls cold water.*

[1] *See* p 83.   [2] *See* Vegetable table, p 38.

143

Put the plums, the ½ teacup water, and sugar into a saucepan and simmer gently until the plums are very soft. Remove the stones and either rub the fruit through a sieve or beat with a wooden spoon until very smooth. Blend the custard powder with a little cold milk, bring the rest of the milk to the boil, pour over the custard, then return to the saucepan and cook until thickened. Cool with a plate over the pan to prevent skin forming. Soften the gelatine in the cold water, and stir this well into the plum pulp (after mashing or sieving). If the plum mixture has become cool you must heat it again, for gelatine is only dissolved by very hot liquid. When the custard and the plum mixtures are nearly cold whisk them very thoroughly together, using an egg whisk if possible. Pour into a mould or basin rinsed out in cold water. When firm turn out.

Light Lunch or Supper

Stuffed Hake Cutlets, with Baked Tomatoes
Chipped Potatoes[1] or Oven-fried Potatoes[2]

Stuffed Hake Cutlets

4 hake cutlets. Salt, pepper. Stuffing.[3] 1 oz margarine. Tomatoes. Lemon and parsley to garnish.

Spread the margarine on a piece of greaseproof paper large enough to cover the top of the dish thoroughly. Put the hake cutlets into a baking dish, sprinkling each piece of fish lightly with salt and pepper. Divide the stuffing between the four cutlets, spreading this over the tops so that you completely cover the fish. Put the greaseproof paper over. If you have room to bake the tomatoes in the same dish do so, failing which use a second dish. Season the tomatoes and put a tiny knob of margarine on each. Bake just above the centre of the oven, in a moderate oven, Mark 4–5 or 350–375 deg. F., for about 20 minutes. Serve garnished with rings of lemon and parsley.

[1] *See* p 118.
[2] *See* p 102.
[3] Recipe, p 141, but use the juice and rind of a whole lemon.

AUGUST THIRD

Main Meal of the Day (Lunch or Dinner)

Crab Mayonnaise
New Potatoes[1]   Green Salad[2]
Caramel Custard

PLAN OF WORK

1. Make Caramel Custard.
2. Put on water for potatoes, then cook these.
3. Dress the crab and make the mayonnaise.
4. Dish up first course.

Crab Mayonnaise

You may find the fishmonger will prepare the crab for you, but generally speaking if you buy already dressed crabs they are more expensive. Preparing a crab takes some little time until you are practised, but it is not difficult. If you fear you may be slow, then it is advisable to do this earlier in the plan of work than is suggested. You will find one medium-sized crab is enough for two people, one large one for four people. Feel the crab when you buy it, and if it feels surprisingly light for its size, ask the fishmonger to break it open – for 'lightness' often indicates that it is 'watery' and you are not getting good solid crab meat. In any case, I would always ask the fishmonger to open the crab to make certain it is quite fresh. When you get it home break the claws with a sharp knock with a hammer. Do this once or twice only, for it makes it a difficult job to remove the meat if you have splintered the shell badly. Use a skewer to remove all the meat from the claws. Open the main part of the shell by pulling up the rounded part. Take out the skin-like 'bag' and the greyish-brown fingers, both of which should be discarded. Remove all white meat and mix with the meat from the claws. Remove the brown meat and keep this separately. If you wish you can crack one or two of the smaller claws as well as the large ones. To make the crab meat go further mix the white meat with a few fine breadcrumbs. Season both white and dark meat, and if everyone likes mayonnaise mix some with it, using about a tablespoonful to the white meat from one medium-sized crab. Wash and dry the crab shell, then

[1] *See* Vegetable table, p 40.   [2] *See* p 68.

fill one side with white meat, and the other side with the dark meat. Put a line of tiny parsley sprigs to divide them. Lay the crab on a bed of prepared lettuce (*see* p 68).

Caramel Custard

FOR THE CARAMEL. *2 oz loaf or granulated sugar. 4 tablespoonfuls water.*

FOR THE CUSTARD. *3 eggs. 1 pint milk. 1 dessertspoonful sugar. ½ oz margarine.*

First make the caramel. Put the sugar and half the water into a small strong saucepan. Stir over a low heat until you can no longer feel the grittiness of the sugar on the bottom of the pan; it is then dissolved. Boil steadily, without stirring, until it turns dark brown. Watch during this process, for it soon turns black and burns. Take the pan off the heat, then add the rest of the water. When you do this the caramel will become a sticky ball, but return to the heat, stir steadily, and it will soon become liquid again. Grease a mould with the margarine. If using a metal mould you can safely pour in the caramel sauce while very hot. With a china or glass basin or mould, it must cool slightly. Wait until the caramel sauce is cold before adding the custard.

To make the custard: pour hot, but not boiling, milk onto the beaten eggs, then add the sugar. Strain over the caramel; this is not essential, but it ensures you have no small pieces of egg floating on top. Cook in the same way as an egg custard (p 127) but as you are using a larger quantity allow twice the time. Cool the caramel custard, and when nearly cold turn out onto a dish. Do not wait until it is quite cold, otherwise some of the caramel will stick to the mould.

Light Lunch or Supper

Stewed Kidneys on Toast

Stewed Kidneys on Toast

4 or 6 lambs' kidneys. 1 oz margarine. ½ oz flour. ¼ pint water or stock. Salt and pepper. 4 slices of hot buttered toast. Parsley.

Cut the kidneys in halves, after first washing them and removing the thin skins. Heat the margarine in a saucepan, and toss the kidneys in this for about 3 minutes. Blend the flour slowly with the stock or water (to which you could add a little Marmite – but don't use too much, otherwise the flavour of the kidneys will be lost). Add the liquid to the kidneys, bring slowly to the boil, then cook gently for about 10 minutes. Season well. Put on toast just before serving, and sprinkle finely chopped parsley on top.

September Shopping

This month is a busy one for most housewives, for it is well worth while making full use of the plentiful supplies of plums (with other fruits of the plum family such as damsons and green-gages), English tomatoes, outdoor cucumbers, and runner beans, which are plentiful. Field mushrooms are available too, and much cheaper than cultivated mushrooms. All these can be preserved for winter use (*see* Section IV), so saving money and adding variety to your menu.

FOODS IN SEASON

Eggs. Supplies should be reasonable during this month.

Fish. Very much the same fish will be available as in August, but salmon is now going out of season. Among white fish skate is a 'bad buy' this month, for it is thin and poor. The oyster season begins again.

Fruit. Plentiful supplies of apples, greengages, plums, Italian clingstone peaches, and damsons in the early part of the month.

Meat. Very often good supplies of pork are available during the next month or so.

Vegetables. Very similar to those available in August, except peas are often poor as they are too old. Runner beans are at their best, so are outdoor tomatoes and cucumbers. Marrows are getting very large, and while suitable to stuff are less good for a vegetable. You may find the first celery in the shops, but it is generally agreed that the flavour is better after the first frosts. Among less usual vegetables is the globe artichoke, delicious if cooked steadily in boiling salted water for about 35 minutes, then served with melted butter. It is, however, an expensive vegetable.

September Meals

SEPTEMBER FIRST

Breakfast

Cereal
Tomatoes on Toast
etc

Tomatoes on Toast

8 medium-sized tomatoes. 2 oz lard or good dripping or bacon fat (saved from frying bacon rinds or cheap fat bacon). Salt, pepper, sugar. 4 slices of hot buttered toast.

Cut the tomatoes into slices about ½ inch thick. Heat the lard in a frying-pan, then fry the sliced tomatoes gently until soft, adding a good pinch salt and pepper and a very small pinch of sugar. Pile onto the hot toast and serve at once.

Main Meal of the Day (Lunch or Dinner)

Roast Veal with Veal Stuffing[1]   Sausages
Runner Beans[2]   Creamed Potatoes[3]
Plum Fool

PLAN OF WORK

1. Make the Plum Fool.
2. Prepare stuffing and vegetables.
3. Put meat and stuffing into oven which has been pre-heated.
4. Add sausages about 45 minutes before meat is cooked.
5. Boil water for vegetables, then put in first potatoes, then beans.
6. Cream potatoes.
7. Make gravy and dish up first course.

Roast Veal and Stuffing

Choose a piece suitable for roasting (*see* p 34).

If using loin, fillet, or shoulder spread the stuffing over the meat, roll tightly, and tie round with string. For best end of neck split down the meat and sandwich the stuffing between the two layers of meat. Put the meat into the baking tin with about

[1] *See* p 141.   [2] *See* Vegetable table, p 38.   [3] *See* p 72.

3 oz dripping or lard, for veal has a tendency to dry easily. Set the oven for hot, Mark 6–7 or 425–450 deg. F., and keep it at this temperature for the first 30 minutes of cooking time. After this the heat can be reduced to Mark 5–6 or 375–400 deg. F. (moderately hot). Put the meat in the hottest part of the oven (*see* diagrams on p 19).

Roast Sausages

Prick the sausages and put around the meat about 45 minutes before this is done.

Plum Fool

¾–1 lb plums (*according to size; a bigger weight of small plums will be needed than of large ones*). 2–3 oz sugar. 1½ level tablespoonfuls custard powder. Few glacé cherries. 2 or 3 tablespoonfuls water. ½ pint milk.

Blend the custard powder with a little cold milk, bring the rest of the milk to the boil, pour over the custard powder, stirring all the time. Return to the saucepan and cook until thickened, adding 1 level tablespoonful of the sugar. While the custard is being made, simmer the plums with the water and rest of the sugar. Remove the stones, and either rub through a sieve or beat into a smooth pulp. When both fruit and custard have cooled slightly, beat together. Put into four glasses and allow to cool. Decorate on top with cherries.

Variations

Blackcurrant. Simmer ¾ lb blackcurrants without water, for you must have a very thick fruit pulp. Rub through a sieve and allow the fruit to get *quite* cold before adding to custard, for blackcurrants have so much acid that the mixture might curdle.

Damson. As blackcurrant.

Gooseberry. Use rather green fruit to give a good flavour, and the same amount of water as for plums. This means stirring the fruit well to begin with, so that it does not burn. Sieve to get rid of pips and skins.

Rhubarb. Use ¾ lb fruit, but simmer in a covered dish in a low oven, so that you need add no water at all. Either sieve or beat with a wooden spoon to a smooth purée.

149

Rich Fruit Fool. Instead of custard use whipped cream or partly custard and partly whipped cream.

Light Lunch or Supper
Cold Veal and Ham
Autumn Salad

Autumn Salad
Include cooked runner beans, peas, rings of apple, quarters of pear stuffed with cream cheese.

SEPTEMBER SECOND

Breakfast
Fruit Juice[1]
Bacon and Mushrooms

Bacon and Mushrooms
Since mushrooms take a little time to cook it is better to fry these before the bacon. To prepare the mushrooms remove the skin, either with your fingertips or the point of a sharp knife. Take out the stalks, but either keep these for adding to soups or stews or fry with the cups of the mushrooms. Wash the mushrooms and dry them well. Put the bacon rinds and about an ounce of dripping or lard into the frying-pan. Heat steadily and then put in the mushrooms. Cook steadily for about 8 minutes. If sliced they take only 5–6 minutes. Lift out with a fish slice, draining over the pan. Keep hot while you fry the bacon (*see* p 75).

Main Meal of the Day (Lunch or Dinner)
Vegetable Soup
Fried Cutlets of Hake or Halibut
Chipped Potatoes[2]   *Fried Cucumber*
Fresh Greengage Pudding

PLAN OF WORK
1. Make the Greengage Pudding.
2. Prepare vegetables, and make soup.
3. Fry potatoes and cucumber.

[1] *See* p 84.   [2] *See* p 118.

4. Fry cutlets of fish.
5. Give potatoes final fry.
6. Drain both fish and potatoes on crumpled paper and keep in oven, while serving the soup.

Vegetable Soup

Use the same recipe as for Potato Soup on p 82, but allow a good mixture of vegetables – carrots, little turnip and/or swede, onion, a tomato, and the mushroom stalks if wished.

Fried Cutlets of Hake or Halibut

Follow directions for coating and frying fish as directed on p 117, but since these cutlets are thick and solid, make certain you cook them sufficiently long. Garnish the cutlets with lemon slices and parsley.

Fried Cucumber

Cucumber is delicious when fried, and outdoor cucumbers are particularly cheap. Peel them and cut into slices. Dry the slices well in a cloth. Dust with flour, to which you add a little salt and pepper. After frying the potatoes for the first time, put in the slices of cucumber and cook for about 4 minutes, until golden brown. Drain on crumpled tissue paper.

Fresh Greengage Pudding

Follow directions for blackcurrant pudding on p 138, but if the fruit is very ripe do not add much water.

Light Lunch or Supper

Stuffed Baked Marrow
Jacket Potatoes[1]

Stuffed Baked Marrow

1 medium-sized marrow or half a very large one.

FOR STUFFING. Use the same mixture as for Durham cutlets or Rissoles (pp 87, 152), but do not form into shapes. Or *2 oz boiled rice. 2–3 oz grated cheese. 1 egg. Salt, pepper. 2 sliced tomatoes. 1 oz margarine.*
About 2 oz fat for roasting the marrow.

[1] *See* p 88.

If you have plenty of time the marrow can be cooked entirely in the oven by roasting, otherwise you can steam it for a short time first. To prepare the marrow remove the skin, cut through the centre lengthwise, and remove the pips. Put into a steamer, sprinkling with salt and pepper, and steam over boiling water for about 8 minutes. Lift out and drain carefully. Press the stuffing into half of the marrow and put the other half on top. Heat the fat in a baking tin, put in the marrow. Baste with the hot fat and cook for about 1 hour in the centre of a moderate to moderately hot oven, Mark 5–6 or 375–400 deg. F. If the marrow has not been steamed allow about 1½ hours, reducing the heat after the first ¾ hour to very moderate, Mark 3–4 or 350–375 deg. F. Lift onto a dish and garnish with parsley.

To make the stuffing No 2: Heat the margarine, fry the sliced tomatoes until softened, stir in the rice, cheese, salt and pepper, and lastly a beaten egg.

SEPTEMBER THIRD

Breakfast
Grapefruit[1]
Bloaters
etc

To Cook Bloaters. These can be cooked in just the same way as kippers except that being thicker (as they are not split open) they take a little longer (*see* p 112). The boiling water method can also be used, and the bloaters then covered with a little margarine and put under a hot grill for about 4 minutes.

Main Meal of the Day (Lunch or Dinner)
Lancashire Hot Pot
Macedoine of Vegetables
Fruit Sponge Pudding

PLAN OF WORK
1. Prepare vegetables for the Hot Pot and Macedoine.
2. Put the hot pot into oven, which has been pre-heated.
3. Make the Fruit Sponge Pudding, and cook this.

[1] *See* p 70.

4. Put on water for vegetables and cook these.
5. Dish up first course.

Lancashire Hot Pot

¾ lb lean best neck of mutton or stewing steak. 2 large onions. 1 lb potatoes. Hot water. Salt, pepper. 1 oz margarine.

Cut the meat into neat pieces, and peel and slice the potatoes and onions; they should be about ¼ inch thick. Fill a casserole with alternate layers of meat, onions, potato. You should end with a layer of potato. Sprinkle salt and pepper over each layer. Pour enough hot water into the casserole to about half fill. Put the margarine on top in small pieces, and put on the lid. If the casserole hasn't a lid, then spread the margarine over greaseproof paper and tuck this securely over the top. Bake in the coolest part of the oven (*see* diagrams, p 19) either for 2 hours at Mark 3 or 325–350 deg. F., or for a good 1½ hours at Mark 4 or 350–375 deg. F. (use the latter temperature if baking a pudding as well). Take lid or paper off for the last 20 minutes to brown the top.

Macedoine of Vegetables

Have as large a mixture of vegetables as possible – carrots, turnips, one or two potatoes (if there are not sufficient in the hot pot), few beans, an onion, or any other variety you have available. Cut the beans into ½-inch lengths and the other vegetables into small dice. Cook in boiling salted water for about 20 minutes. Drain and serve with chopped parsley on top.

Fruit Sponge Pudding

Approximately ¾ lb fruit. Little water. Sugar or syrup to taste (about 2 oz).

FOR THE SPONGE. *2–3 oz margarine. 2–3 oz sugar. ½ egg. 4 oz flour (with plain flour use 1 teaspoonful baking powder). 1 tablespoonful water if using 3 oz margarine or 1½ tablespoonfuls water for 2 oz margarine.*

All fruits except pears are suitable; apples should be sliced, plums unless small should be halved. Put the fruit at the bottom of the pie dish, with sugar and just enough water to cover the bottom of the dish. Next make the sponge mixture.

Cream together the margarine and sugar with a wooden spoon until the mixture is very soft and light-coloured. Stir in the egg, the flour, and water, taking care not to over-beat. You will notice that the mixture is slightly stiffer than that for a steamed sponge pudding, but this is advisable because the fruit underneath is inclined to soften the sponge. Spread over the fruit. Bake about the middle of a very moderate oven (*see* diagrams, p 19), Mark 3–4 or 325–350 deg. F., for about 50 minutes. If the top is becoming a little too brown, then lower the heat gradually. Make sure the pudding is well on the way to being cooked before you open the oven door to remove the hot pot.

Light Lunch or Supper

Grilled Herrings in Oatmeal
Grilled Tomatoes

Grilled Herrings in Oatmeal

4 large or 8 small herrings. 2 tablespoonfuls medium ground oatmeal. Good pinch salt and pepper. 4 large tomatoes. 1 oz margarine. Lemon, parsley.

Halve the tomatoes, put into the grill pan, with a sprinkling of salt and pepper and little margarine on top. Mix a good pinch salt and pepper with the oatmeal. Prepare the herrings (*see* p 123), making three slits on top with a sharp knife to prevent the skin curling badly. Roll the herrings thickly in the oatmeal. Put on the grid over the tomatoes, and under the hot grill. Cook quickly for about 4 minutes, turn, then cook for the same length of time on the under side. Reduce heat and cook steadily for a further 3–4 minutes. Garnish with the tomatoes, rings of lemon, and parsley.

October Shopping

Now is the time to make your Christmas puddings if you have not already done so (*see* Christmas Catering, p 182).

The fruits and vegetables available this month depend very much on the weather. If the nights are severe then there will be few runner beans. Those of you living near the country will be able to gather blackberries and the last of the field mushrooms, but do make certain, whether you pick these yourself, or buy them from shops, that they *are* mushrooms and not some dangerous fungi. The top should be smooth and the stalk firm; the underside of young mushrooms is pink, of older ones dark brown.

FOODS IN SEASON

Fish. WHITE FISH. The list varies little from August and September. Turbot is at its worst, but cod much better. OILY FISH. Mackerel should be considered out of season until next April, but herrings are still good. They are really the only oily type of fish you can rely upon. SHELLFISH. Most shellfish is not at its best; oysters should be excellent, but crab and crawfish are less good. Lobster and shrimps are still available.

Fruit. Cooking apples, eating apples, blackberries, oranges, pears and last of the plums.

Vegetables. GREEN VEGETABLES. Brussels sprouts (though rather expensive), cabbage, cauliflower, kale, mushrooms, spinach (generally excellent) all available. You may still obtain globe artichokes, but season is ending. ROOT VEGETABLES. Artichokes (Jerusalem), carrots, celery, chicory, onions, parsnips, swedes, turnips.

Other foods. As for September, p 147.

October Meals

OCTOBER FIRST

Breakfast
Porridge[1]
Bacon and Tomatoes
etc

Bacon and Tomatoes

You will find instructions for cooking bacon on p 75 and for frying tomatoes on p 80, but always cook the bacon first, since tomatoes are so 'watery' they are inclined to cause bacon to stick to the bottom of the pan.

[1] *See* p 60.

Main Meal of the Day (Lunch or Dinner)

Steak and Kidney Pie
Jerusalem Artichokes[1]   Potatoes[1]
Baked Stuffed Apples

PLAN OF WORK

1. Make pastry for the Steak and Kidney Pie.
2. Put this into oven, pre-heated.
3. Prepare apples and put into oven.
4. Prepare vegetables, and put on water for these.
5. Cook vegetables and dish up first course.

Steak and Kidney Pie

¾– 1 lb stewing steak. 2 lamb's or sheep's kidneys or about 4 oz ox kidney. 1 level tablespoonful flour. Good pinch pepper. ½ teaspoonful salt. Water or stock. Short-crust or flaky pastry.

For short-crust pastry, *see* recipe on p 65.

Make sure you can make good short-crust pastry (which is the more useful) before embarking on the flaky type, which is more difficult and takes longer.

For flaky pastry use *6 oz flour (preferably plain). 4 oz fat (preferably 3 oz margarine and 1 oz lard). Good pinch salt. Cold water to mix.*

First prepare the pastry. To make flaky pastry: sieve flour and salt together. Rub in one-third of the fat. Mix to a firm dough with the water. Roll out to an oblong shape. Divide the rest of the fat into half. Put half on the dough in small pieces, *covering two-thirds* of the dough, and leaving the bottom third without any fat. Bring up this third, and fold over half the fat, then bring down the top half. If you make the dough look first like an opened envelope, then like a closed envelope, you are folding correctly. Turn the pastry, seal the edges – to keep in the air – and rib it (ie, depress at intervals) with the rolling pin, then roll out again. Repeat this process with the rest of the fat then turn, seal the edges, rib, and re-roll. Do this twice more, then the pastry is ready to use. If time permits, put it into a cold place between rolling and using; always do so when using it for a pie.

[1] *See* Vegetable table, pp 38, 40.

156

Don't worry if the pastry appears to be getting rather sticky. Put it away, then bring out after about 30 minutes.

To prepare the meat for the pie: cut the steak and kidney into small pieces, and roll in the flour, to which add the salt and pepper. Stand a pie support or egg cup in the dish in the centre to support the pastry. Put the meat into the pie dish, seeing that the kidney is well distributed. Pour over enough water or stock to come halfway up the meat – any more would boil out in cooking.

Roll out the pastry and cover the pie (as directed on p 87). If you have any scraps of pastry left form these into leaves and a rose to decorate the pie; it is traditional in cookery to orna-ment savoury pies in this way and not sweet ones. To make leaves, roll out the pastry to a strip, then cut leaf shapes (approxi-mately diamond) marking the 'veins' with the point of a knife. To make a rose, cut a narrow strip, then roll this round, and with your fingertips depress at intervals to give petal shape. Brush the top of the pie over with a very little milk, sticking the leaves and rose into position. Make a tiny slit in the pastry over the pie support or egg cup, to allow the steam to escape. Bake in the centre of a hot oven, Mark 6–7 or 425–450 deg. F., for about 25 minutes to give the pastry a chance to rise, then put a piece of paper over the top and lower the heat to very moderate, Mark 3 or 325–350 deg. F., to make sure the meat is cooked. Give it about a further 1½ hours. When serving, have a sauceboat of hot stock available to pour into the pie to make extra gravy if you wish.

Baked Stuffed Apples

4 large cooking apples. FOR THE STUFFING: *2 tablespoonfuls golden syrup or honey. 2 tablespoonfuls sultanas or currants. 1 tablespoonful breadcrumbs. 9 oz margarine.*

Wash and dry the apples then, using a sharp knife, split the skin round the centre; this makes it very easy to remove when the apples are cooked. Using an apple corer take out the cores. Stand the apples in a baking tin or dish, then divide the syrup between them, pouring this into the centre hole. Add the fruit, breadcrumbs, and a tiny knob of margarine on top of each. Bake for approximately 1 hour in a very moderate oven, Mark 3 or 325–350 deg. F. Serve with any liquid in the dish and cream or the top of the milk or custard (made according to directions on the packet).

Light Lunch or Supper

Vegetable Soup[1]
Scotch Woodcock

Scotch Woodcock

4 slices buttered toast. 4–5 eggs. 1 oz margarine. Salt, pepper. 2 tablespoonfuls milk. 8 fillets of anchovy.

Beat the eggs, adding salt, pepper, and milk. Heat the margarine in a saucepan and scramble the eggs as directed on p 81. Pile onto the toast and serve with the 2 fillets of anchovy neatly crossed on top of each piece of toast. (Fillets of anchovy are sold in tins.) If you wish to cook the eggs slowly while eating the soup do these in a basin over hot water or a double saucepan, when they won't stick or dry.

OCTOBER SECOND

Breakfast

Cereal
Sausage and Potato Cakes
etc

Sausage and Potato Cakes

½ lb sausage meat. ½ lb mashed potato. 1 dessertspoonful chopped parsley. 1 egg. Good pinch mixed herbs. Little flour. 1–2 oz lard or dripping.

Mix the potato and sausage meat together, adding all the other ingredients. Form into 8 flat round cakes, then roll in flour. This can be done the night before. Heat the lard and fry the cakes steadily until brown on one side, turn and brown steadily the other side, then lower the heat and cook gently for about 5 minutes. Drain with a fish slice and serve at once.

Main Meal of the Day (Lunch or Dinner)

Tripe and Onions
Creamed Potatoes[2]   *Spinach*[3]
Blackberry and Apple Crunch

[1] *See* pp 82, 89.   [2] *See* p 72.   [3] *See* Vegetable table, p 41.

1. Prepare the vegetables.
2. Blanch the tripe, then put on to cook.
3. Prepare the fruit crunch and put in oven.
4. Put on water for vegetables, and cook these.
5. Thicken tripe.
6. Dish up first course.

Tripe and Onions

1¼–1½ lb tripe. 3 large onions. Salt, pepper. 1 oz margarine. 1 oz flour. ½ pint milk.

Cut the tripe into neat strips. Put these into cold water, bring the water to the boil, and strain it away. This initial process known as 'blanching' improves both colour and smell of the tripe. Put the tripe back into the saucepan with the sliced onions, salt and pepper, and barely enough water to half cover. Put on the lid of the pan, bring slowly to boiling point, turn down the heat, and simmer gently for about an hour. Blend the flour with the milk and add to the tripe, together with the margarine. Bring to the boil, stirring all the time, then cook gently for about 15 minutes. Serve dusted with paprika pepper, and, if you have time, garnished with small triangles of buttered toast, for the crispness of the toast is a pleasing contrast to the soft tripe.

Blackberry and Apple Crunch

½ lb blackberries. Little water. Approximately ¾ lb cooking apples. About 2 oz sugar or golden syrup.

For the crunch: *2 oz margarine. 2 level tablespoonfuls golden syrup. 1 breakfast cup cornflakes.*

Peel and core the apples and cut into thin slices. Put them and the blackberries into a pie dish together with the sugar or golden syrup and about a teacup water. Cook in a very low oven, Mark 2 or 300–325 deg. F., for about 25 minutes. Heat the syrup and margarine together in a saucepan until the margarine has melted, stir in the cornflakes. Spread this sticky mixture on top of the hot fruit, then return to the oven for a further 30 minutes.

Light Lunch or Supper

Savoury Spaghetti
Stewed Mushrooms

Savoury Spaghetti

3–4 oz spaghetti (or macaroni). 1 teaspoonful salt. 3 large tomatoes. 1 large onion. 2 oz margarine. 3 tablespoonfuls grated cheese. Salt, pepper.

Bring 1½ pints water to the boil, add the salt, then when the water is boiling put in the spaghetti or macaroni. Cook steadily for about 7 minutes for spaghetti or 10 minutes for macaroni. Drain carefully. Heat the margarine in a pan, then fry the slices of tomato and onion until soft. Stir in the spaghetti, adding extra seasoning and half the cheese. When very hot pile into a hot dish, and shake over the rest of the cheese.

Stewed Mushrooms

Approximately 6 oz mushrooms. 1½ teacups milk. 1 dessertspoonful flour. ½ oz margarine. Salt, pepper.

Prepare the mushrooms (*see* p 150). Put them into a saucepan with a gill of milk, and a good shake of salt and pepper. Simmer gently (with a lid on the pan) for about 8 minutes. Blend the flour carefully with the ½ gill cold milk and stir into the mushrooms, adding the margarine. Bring steadily to the boil and stir for a few minutes until thickened slightly. Serve separately or round the dish of spaghetti.

Mushrooms on Toast. You can either fry the mushrooms (*see* p 150) or cook them in this way before putting on toast or using them as a filling to an omelet.

OCTOBER THIRD

Breakfast

Porridge[1]
Tomato Omelet
etc

Tomato Omelet

For the omelet follow directions on p 120. Slice the tomatoes (allowing one for each person). Heat 1 oz lard or dripping in a saucepan or second frying-pan and cook the tomatoes until just soft, adding a good pinch salt and pepper. When the omelets are just firm fill with tomatoes and fold, away from the handle. Turn onto a hot dish.

[1] *See* p 60.

Main Meal of the Day (Lunch or Dinner)

Haricot Mutton
Braised Onions   Mashed Swedes[1]
Damson Snow

PLAN OF WORK

1. Cook damsons, sieve these, and cool.
2. Prepare vegetables.
3. Put on Haricot Mutton, the haricot beans having been soaked overnight.
4. Cook braised onions.
5. Put on water for swedes, and cook these.
6. Add sliced potatoes to Haricot Mutton.
7. Complete Damson Snow.
8. Dish up first course.

Haricot Mutton

1 lb mutton. 4 small carrots. 1 large onion. 6 oz haricot beans. 1 oz flour. 1 oz lard or dripping. 1 pint water or stock. Salt, pepper. Few potatoes.

The mutton should be as lean as possible. Choose best end of neck or leg, or shoulder. If you have a large piece of leg or shoulder for roasting, it is a good idea to cut some slices for this dish before cooking.

Soak haricot beans overnight in cold water, leaving plenty of room in the container for the beans to swell. Heat the lard in the saucepan and fry the sliced onions and meat cut into neat pieces, for a few minutes. Stir in the flour and cook this gently for about 5 minutes, stirring all the time. Gradually add the cold stock or water, bring to the boil – stir well until the stock has boiled and thicken slightly. Add the carrots, salt and pepper, and haricot beans, well drained. Simmer gently for nearly 2 hours. Slice the potatoes, which could be omitted if you are serving onions and swedes, for the haricot beans adequately take their place in this dish. Put the potatoes, with seasoning, on top of the mutton stew, adding a good pinch salt and pepper. Cook for a further 25 minutes until the potatoes are tender. To dish up lift the sliced potatoes carefully from the stew, put these on a hot

[1] *See p 77.*

dish, pour the haricot mutton on top. Finish the dish with sprigs
of parsley.

Braised Onions

4 medium-sized onions. 1 oz lard. 1 oz flour. ½ pint water or stock.
  Salt, pepper.

Peel the onions, but keep them whole. Heat the lard in a saucepan
then toss the onions in this for several minutes until slightly
brown on the outside. Stir the flour into the fat, and cook well
for a few minutes. It is advisable to remove the onions onto a
plate while doing this. Gradually stir in the cold water or stock,
bring the sauce to the boil, and cook for about 5 minutes, until
thick, add salt and pepper to taste, and a very little Marmite or
Bovril to give colour and extra flavour to the dish if you are using
water. Put in the onions and either cook over a *very low* heat,
with the lid on the saucepan, for just over an hour or, if you are
using the oven, transfer to a covered casserole and cook in a
very moderate oven, Mark 3 or 325–350 deg. F., for just over an
hour. The sauce becomes very thick and coats the onions.

Damson Snow

1 lb damsons. 1 teacup water. 2 oz sugar. 2 egg whites.

Put the damsons, water, and sugar into a saucepan and simmer
gently until the fruit is very soft. Rub through a sieve to remove
stones and skin. Allow to cool, taste the mixture – for damsons
can be very sour – and if necessary stir in a little more sugar.
Whisk the egg whites until very stiff, then *fold* (*see* p 49) very
gently into the damson mixture. Pile in four glasses.
Note. The egg yolks can be used for the kedgeree (*see* p 163).

Variations

Apple. Cook the apples with about ½ teacup water, and a little
lemon juice to flavour. The apple pulp could be coloured pale
pink by putting in *one or two drops* of cochineal (*see* p 23).

Blackberry. Cook the fruit with no water, just sugar. Sieve and
cool, then fold in egg whites.

Blackcurrant. As Blackberry.

Gooseberry. Use 1 teacup water if the fruit is under-ripe, but
only ½ teacup if ripe.

Raspberry. Do not cook the fruit. Sieve if wished, or just mash, adding sugar to taste. Stir in the egg whites.

Strawberry. As Raspberry.

Light Lunch or Supper
Mushroom Soup
Kedgeree

Mushroom Soup

½ lb mushrooms, or stalks. 1 pint water or stock. 1 oz flour. 2 oz margarine. Salt, pepper.

Many large greengrocer's shops stock mushroom stalks, which are very much cheaper of course than whole mushrooms. These are ideal for soups. Wash and skin the mushrooms (*see* p 150), although if cultivated mushrooms – not the field type – the skins can be left on if the mushrooms are well washed. Cut into small pieces about the size of a small fingernail. Heat the margarine, then fry the mushrooms for about 5 minutes, taking care they do not dry badly or discolour. Stir in the flour and cook for about another 5 minutes, then gradually add the cold stock or water. Bring to the boil and cook until slightly thickened, adding a good pinch salt and pepper. Reduce the heat and simmer gently for 10 minutes.

Kedgeree

3 oz boiled rice (p 98). 1 large cooked Finnan Haddock (see p 70). 1 hard-boiled egg. Little milk or egg yolks. 2 oz margarine. Salt, pepper.

To garnish (this is not essential): *2 or 3 large onions. Deep fat for frying, or 2–4 oz lard. Thick batter (see p 117) or little milk and flour.*

Flake all the fish from the haddock, removing skin and bones. Heat the margarine in a saucepan, stir in the fish, rice, and just enough milk or egg yolks to make a sticky consistency. (The egg yolks left over from the Damson Snow could be used.) Add salt and pepper to taste, remembering smoked haddock is already rather salt. Heat through gently. Pile into a hot dish, and garnish with chopped hard-boiled egg. Serve at once.

The correct garnish is hard-boiled egg and fried onions. You may like to try this when you have mastered the art of frying onions properly.

To fry onions (for both crisp and soft outsides): peel the onions and cut into rings across the centre. Put these into a cloth and dry thoroughly; this is important. To fry in shallow fat, brush the onions with a little milk, then toss in flour, to which you add a good pinch salt and pepper. Make sure the fat is very hot (*see* p 117). Put in the onions and fry until *crisp and brown*. Drain on crumpled tissue paper.

For soft-fried onions cook more slowly and dish up when tender. For deep frying, dry the onion rings, then dip in the thick batter. Have the pan of fat smoking hot, and test as for frying potatoes (*see* p 118). Put in the onions, fry until really crisp and golden coloured. Drain on crumpled tissue paper.

November Shopping

As this month often means the beginning of real winter, it is important to plan your meals to give good sustaining, satisfying meals. At the same time don't neglect salads and fruits, for winter vegetables can make excellent salads, particularly if you include fruit to give colour and interest. Good feeding at this time of the year may take your family through the winter without colds or flu. Start to collect dried fruit, etc, for Christmas catering.

FOODS IN SEASON

Eggs. You may find eggs expensive, so if you were wise enough to preserve some in the spring this is the time to start using them.

Fish. WHITE FISH. Much the same as in the earlier autumn months (*see* August list, p 139). Cod and haddock are now available, and should be excellent. Turbot much better. OILY FISH. Again much the same as August, but sprats will be available, and these tiny fish are full of flavour and nourishment. SHELLFISH. Lobsters, oysters, shrimps.

Fruit. While there should be many apples and pears, most of the fruit in the shops at this time of the year is imported.

Meat. Plentiful supply of all meat and poultry.

Vegetables. As October, but brussels sprouts more plentiful, and celeriac and seakale may be available to add to list of root vegetables.

November Meals

NOVEMBER FIRST

Breakfast

Grapefruit[1]
Sardines on Toast
etc

Sardines on Toast

Pre-heat the grill to make the toast. Butter toast lightly, since sardines are very oily. Arrange sardines on the toast, and heat through gently in a very low oven or under a very low grill.

Main Meal of the Day (Lunch or Dinner)

Roast Rabbit with Sage and Onion Stuffing (if wished)
Braised Celery   Roast Jacket Potatoes
Apple and Date Plate Tart

PLAN OF WORK

1. Make pastry and prepare fruit tart. Soak rabbit.
2. Prepare vegetables.
3. Make stuffing and put rabbit into oven, pre-heated.
4. Put potatoes in fat round the rabbit, and celery into casserole.
5. Cook plate tart.
6. Dish up first course.

Roast Rabbit

1 small young rabbit. Sage and onion stuffing.[2] *2 or 3 rashers of bacon. Fat for roasting.*

Soak the rabbit for about 2 hours in vinegar and water (1 table-spoonful vinegar to a pint cold water). This improves both colour and flavour. Wash the rabbit in fresh water and dry it. Put the stuffing into the rabbit, and lay the rashers of bacon on

[1] *See* p 70.   [2] *See* p 64.

top. Stand in the roasting tin, with 2–4 oz dripping. Cook for about 1½ hours, starting in a hot oven, Mark 6–7 or 425–450 deg. F., for the first 25–30 minutes, then reducing the heat to moderately hot, Mark 6 or 400–425 deg. F.

The flavour of rabbit when roasted is excellent, provided it is well cooked, and you have been careful to choose a young rabbit.

Roast Jacket Potatoes

Choose medium-sized potatoes, as near same size as possible, and with unblemished skins. Scrub the skins and dry thoroughly. Roast for about 1 hour, turning round in the hot fat, so that each potato is well coated. The flavour of both skins and the potato inside is delicious.

Braised Celery

Wash the head of celery well, then divide into neat pieces about 3 inches in length. Allow ¼ of the heart for each person, and some of the outside sticks. With a big head of celery you could eat the heart and just cook the outside sticks, provided they are firm and good. Braise in exactly the same way as for braised onions (*see* p 181), putting the casserole in the coolest part of the oven when using it for roasting. Cook for about 45–50 minutes.

Apple and Date Plate Tart

SHORT-CRUST PASTRY. *8 oz flour. 4 oz fat (preferably 2 oz margarine and 2 oz lard). Good pinch salt. Cold water to mix.*

FILLING. *Approximately ½ lb apples (weight when peeled). ½ tablespoonful sugar. 3 oz dates. Pinch mixed spice.*

Make the pastry according to direction on p 71. Roll out and cut a round large enough to cover one 7- or 8-inch baking plate. Slice the apples thinly and dry them well, otherwise the bottom pastry will be 'soggy'. Arrange the apples and chopped dates over the pastry. There is no need to buy the expensive dessert dates – use the cheaper block stoned dates. Sprinkle the sugar and spice over them. Roll out the rest of the pastry to a round large enough to cover. Brush the edges of both rounds with water, seal together, by pinching hard, then press round with a fork. This both seals the edges more thoroughly, and gives a decorative appearance. Bake for about 45 minutes in the centre of a

166

moderately hot oven, Mark 6 or 400–425 deg. F. Reduce heat after 20 minutes. Do not use the hottest part of the oven, otherwise the top pastry is over-cooked before the filling and bottom layer of pastry is cooked.

Light Lunch or Supper

Baked Sausages and Tomatoes
Scalloped Potatoes

Baked Sausages and Tomatoes

Heat 1 oz lard in a baking tin or dish. Prick the sausages and put into this. Cook for 25–30 minutes in a moderately hot oven for small sausages, 40–45 minutes for larger ones. Add the halved tomatoes to the dish about 15 minutes before the sausages are cooked.

Scalloped Potatoes

4 very large potatoes. 1 teacup milk. 1–2 oz margarine. Salt, pepper. Chopped parsley.

Peel the potatoes and slice them rather thinly. Grease a dish and arrange the slices in it, seasoning well. Heat the milk, pour over the potatoes. Put the margarine on top and bake for about 45 minutes in a moderate to moderately hot oven, Mark 5–6 or 425 deg. F. Garnish with the chopped parsley.

Note. These are equally good if cooked much more slowly, ie, about 1½–2 hours in a very low oven, Mark 1–2 or 275–300 deg. F.

NOVEMBER SECOND

Breakfast

Cold Sliced Boiled Bacon[1]
Sliced Tomatoes
etc

Main Meal of the Day (Lunch or Dinner)

Braised Hearts
Macedoine of Vegetables[2]   Savoury Creamed Potatoes
Fairy Puddings   Custard Sauce

[1] *See* p 110.   [2] *See* p 153.

1. Prepare the vegetables.
2. Commence cooking Braised Hearts.
3. Make the pudding and start to steam it.
4. Put on water for the vegetables, start to cook these.
5. Cream potatoes, add parsley, etc.
6. Make Custard Sauce and keep it warm.
7. Dish up first course.

Braised Hearts

2–3 sheep's hearts or ¾ lb ox heart. 1 oz lard. 1 oz flour. 1 onion. ½ pint stock, or water flavoured with little Marmite or Bovril. Salt, pepper.

Wash the hearts thoroughly, then cut into slices about ½ inch thick. Heat the lard, then fry the sliced onion and heart for a few minutes. Stir in the flour and cook for about 5 minutes. Gradually stir in the cold stock or water, bring to the boil, and cook until thickened slightly. Add salt and pepper. Put the lid on the pan and simmer gently for about 1½ hours. Dish up garnished with a little of the macedoine of vegetables.

Savoury Creamed Potatoes

1 lb creamed potatoes (see p 72). 1 tablespoonful chopped parsley. 2 teaspoonfuls chopped chives (when available). Good pinch mixed herbs. A shaking of celery salt.

Fairy Puddings

Follow directions for sponge pudding (p 77), but omit the marmalade. Add instead about 4 oz sultanas or currants. These should be well washed and dried. It is advisable to wash all dried fruit when you receive it from the grocer, so that it has a good chance to dry slowly in the warm air of the kitchen (on flat dishes). If it is too moist when used in cakes and puddings it will spoil them. After 48 hours the fruit is dry, and can be put into a tin or jar. When you have mixed the pudding put it either into one greased basin and steam (see p 78) or into four small basins or old cups, and steam for just over 30 minutes. Turn out and serve with hot custard sauce. You will find suggestions for keeping this hot on p 95.

Light Lunch or Supper

Poached Eggs au gratin
Creamed Spinach

Poached Eggs au Gratin

½ *pint cheese sauce (see* p 73). *4 eggs. 2 tablespoonfuls grated cheese.*

It is advisable to cook the cheese sauce before you poach the eggs. These should be cooked according to directions on p 115. To dish up this supper meal arrange the creamed spinach in a dish with the four poached eggs on top. Pour the cheese sauce over, sprinkle the grated cheese on top and brown under a hot grill for a few minutes. Serve at once.

NOVEMBER THIRD

Breakfast

Oslo Breakfast

At this time of the year, when one is inclined to have rather a lot of cooked hot meals, a light yet nutritious meal to start the day (*see* p 109) makes a change and is very beneficial.

Main Meal of the Day (Lunch or Dinner)

Savoury Mincemeat
Celery   Potatoes
Apple Dumplings

PLAN OF WORK

1. Make pastry for Apple Dumplings and prepare these.
2. Prepare vegetables.
3. Start cooking the Savoury Mincemeat, then transfer this to casserole if wished.
4. Cook dumplings.
5. Put on water for vegetables, and cook these.
6. Dish up first course.

Savoury Mincemeat

1 lb freshly minced stewing beef (or minced left-over meat). 2 large onions. 2 small tomatoes. 1 small apple (not essential). ½ pint

169

stock or water. 1 oz lard. 1 oz flour. Salt, pepper. 1 teaspoonful Worcester sauce.

Heat the lard in a saucepan, then fry the sliced onions and tomatoes. If using an apple, shred this into thin slices, and toss in the fat also. Add the mincemeat, then blend the flour with the stock and add to the other ingredients. Bring to the boil, adding good pinch salt and pepper, and the Worcester sauce. If this boils quickly you will find the meat becomes very hard and uninteresting looking, so transfer to a casserole and cook for about 45 minutes in the coolest part of the oven, for this must be moderately hot – Mark 6 or 400–425 deg. F. – for cooking the dumplings. If cooking in a saucepan turn the heat very low for about the same length of time. If you are not cooking apple dumplings the oven need only be at Mark 3 or 325–350 deg. F. Cooked meat needs only about 25 minutes cooking.

Apple Dumplings

4 good-sized cooking apples. Little sugar. 4 cloves, if liked, or pinch of spice.

SHORT-CRUST PASTRY: *8 oz flour, preferably plain. 4 oz fat (preferably 2 oz margarine, 2 oz lard). Pinch salt. Cold water.*

Make the pastry according to directions on p 65, then roll out thinly (not more than $\frac{1}{4}$ inch) and cut into four large squares. Peel and core the apples and stand one apple in the centre of each piece of pastry. Fill the centre core with sugar and put a clove in the very middle, otherwise a pinch of spice. Pick up the corners of each square of pastry and bring these to the middle. Moisten the edges with a little water and bring them together. Stand on a greased baking tin and bake for about 45 minutes just above the middle of a moderately hot oven, Mark 6 or 400–425 deg. F. Reduce heat after 15 minutes.

Boiled Apple Dumplings

Instead of short-crust pastry, use suet crust pastry (*see* p 71), making up 8 oz flour, 4 oz suet, etc. Wrap each dumpling in a clean cloth and steam for about 2 hours in a steamer above rapidly boiling water. Remove the cloth and serve dusted with sugar.

Variations

Apple and Mincemeat. Fill centre hole with mincemeat.

Orange. Peel an orange and sprinkle it lightly with sugar.

Pear. Peel and core a pear, fill centre with sugar and spice.

December and Christmas Catering

This month is probably the busiest if you are entertaining for Christmas. To help you is a 'plan of campaign' (*see* p 179) so that even a beginner in the kitchen will, I hope, find the day goes smoothly. Make Christmas puddings, cake, and mincemeat early in the month, if not already prepared, so that they are out of the way. If properly made they will keep for weeks, or even months.

FOODS IN SEASON

Eggs. These are still expensive, so any eggs you have preserved will come in handy.

Fish. With bad weather you may find fish expensive and selection limited. The varieties are much the same as the autumn months, ie, WHITE FISH. Cod, haddock, hake, halibut, skate, sole, turbot. OILY FISH. Herrings, sprats. SHELLFISH. Crayfish, oysters.

Fruit. Imported fruits such as bananas, grapefruit, oranges are plentiful. English apples excellent. Christmas nuts, dried fruit, tangerines.

Meat. Poultry will be needed in most households for Christmas, but you may prefer to have a good piece of beef or pork instead. Both are excellent at this time of the year.

Vegetables. See November list, p 165.

December Meals

DECEMBER FIRST

Breakfast

Cereal
Stuffed Rolls
etc

171

Stuffed Rolls

Cut the tops off crusty rolls and remove the centre, which can be used for breadcrumbs (*see* p 55). Carefully break an egg inside, dusting this with salt and pepper. Put into a moderately hot oven, Mark 6 or 400–425 deg. F., for about 7 minutes until the egg is only just set.

Main Meal of the Day (Lunch or Dinner)

Stewed Steak and Dumplings
Red Cabbage   Boiled Potatoes[1]
Cabinet Pudding

PLAN OF WORK

1. Prepare vegetables.
2. Cook Stewed Steak.
3. Prepare Cabinet Pudding and start to cook this.
4. Boil water for potatoes, cook these.
5. Boil water for cabbage and make the dumplings, adding these to stewed steak.
6. Cook cabbage.
7. Dish up first course.

Stewed Steak and Dumplings

Cut the steak into neat fingers. Cook it exactly as the haricot mutton (p 161), except that you do not include the haricot beans. At the end of nearly 2 hours make the dumplings (*see* p 77) and add these to the stewed steak, making sure the liquid is boiling steadily. If the liquid has boiled away, put in about another teacup of water, and bring this to the boil, before adding the dumplings. To dish up put the stewed steak in the centre of a hot dish with the dumplings round.

Red Cabbage

This makes a nice change from ordinary greens or cabbage. Cook as any green vegetables (*see* table, p 39). After straining return to the saucepan with about an ounce of margarine, a pinch spice (if you like this) and a pinch sugar. Serve at once.

[1] *See* Vegetable table, p 41.

172

Cabinet Pudding

Follow the directions for bread and butter pudding (p 119), using about an extra ounce of dried fruit or candied peel. Instead of putting the bread and butter, etc, into a pie dish put it into a greased pudding basin. Cover with greased paper and steam over hot water (as for Egg Custard, p 127) for about 1¼ hours.

DECEMBER SECOND

Breakfast

Porridge[1]
Fish and Tomato Cakes
etc

Fish and Tomato Cakes

½ lb cooked flaked fish. ½ lb mashed potato[2]. *2 large tomatoes. Salt, pepper. 1 tablespoonful flour. 2 oz lard or dripping.*

Skin the tomatoes. To do this dip them into boiling water for about 30 seconds, then immediately put them into cold water. Chop up the tomatoes. Mix with the fish, potato, and salt and pepper. If the mixture is very soft add a little flour, but try to avoid this. It won't be necessary if you drain the fish well and use only a little milk to mash the potatoes.

Form into 8 flat cakes, coat with flour, and fry as for fish cakes (*see* p 93).

Main Meal of the Day (Lunch or Dinner)

Liver Casserole
Oven-baked Carrots
Treacle Milk Pudding

PLAN OF WORK

1. Prepare vegetables.
2. Put casserole into the oven, together with carrots.
3. Put in milk pudding.
4. Dish up first course.

Liver Casserole

1 lb calf's or ox liver. 2 tomatoes. 1 lb potatoes. 2 rashers of bacon. 1 tablespoonful flour. 1 oz margarine. ½ pint stock or water. Salt, pepper.

[1] *See p 60.*   [2] *See p 72.*

173

Calf's liver is more tender and moist than ox liver. Cut the liver into neat pieces. Mix a good pinch salt and pepper with the flour and roll the liver in this.

Peel the potatoes, slice, and put a layer at the bottom of the casserole (season it well), then put a layer of liver, then of sliced tomato and chopped rasher of bacon. Add a second layer of potato, liver, tomato, and bacon. Finish with a layer of potato. Each layer of potato should be well seasoned. Pour the liquid over, put the margarine on top, and cover with a lid. Bake for about 2 hours in a very moderate oven, Mark 3 or 325–350 deg. F. If you wish you can remove the lid for the last 20 minutes to brown the top.

Oven-baked Carrots

Cut the carrots into fairly thick slices. Put into a casserole with salt, pepper, $\frac{1}{2}$ teacup water, and about 1 oz margarine. Cover with a lid or paper to stop moisture evaporating. Cook for $1\frac{1}{2}$–2 hours in a very moderate oven, Mark 3 or 325–350 deg. F.

Treacle Milk Pudding

Make as the Rice Pudding on p 122, but add a good tablespoonful black treacle or golden syrup and 2 tablespoonfuls chopped dates. Cook for about $1\frac{1}{2}$–2 hours in the coolest part of a very moderate oven, Mark 3 or 325–350 deg. F.

Light Lunch or Supper

Stuffed Onions
Jacket Potatoes au gratin

Stuffed Onions

4 large onions.

For the stuffing: *4 rashers of bacon or 2 oz chopped ham. $\frac{1}{2}$ teacup breadcrumbs. $\frac{1}{2}$ teaspoonful dried sage. Salt, pepper. 2 eggs. 2 tomatoes. 2 oz margarine, or shredded suet.*

Peel the onions, then put into boiling salted water and cook *steadily* for about 40 minutes. Remove from the water, drain, and take out most of the centre. Chop this finely.

The onions could be cooked up to this point earlier in the day if wished, for it is certainly easier to chop the centre when it is not too hot. Mix the chopped onion with the finely chopped ham or bacon and the rest of the ingredients. The margarine should be beaten well into the mixture, or the suet just added, the eggs beaten well, and the tomatoes skinned (*see* p 173) and chopped. Pile this mixture into the centre of each onion and stand them in a greased dish. Bake for about 45 minutes in a moderate oven, Mark 4–5 or 350–375 deg. F. The stuffing keeps the onions moist, but you can cover the dish with greased paper or a lid if you wish.

Jacket Potatoes au Gratin

Scrub the potatoes and cook as directions on p 88. When cooked, split, remove the centre part of the potato, mash this well. To 4 large potatoes add a good oz margarine, 2 oz grated cheese, salt, and pepper. Pile the mixture back into the potato cases and keep hot until ready.

DECEMBER THIRD

Breakfast
Fruit Juice[1]
Scrambled Eggs with Ham
etc

Scrambled Eggs with Ham

Follow directions for scrambled eggs on p 81, adding about 2 oz finely chopped cooked ham to the melted margarine, and heating for a few minutes before putting in the eggs.

Main Meal of the Day (Lunch or Dinner)
Oxtail Soup
Grilled Sole
Creamed Potatoes[2]
Apple Fritters

PLAN OF WORK

1. Prepare the Oxtail Soup.
2. Make batter and let this stand.

[1] *See* p 84.   [2] *See* p 72.

3. Put on water for potatoes, when boiling start to cook these.
4. Prepare the apples, and fry the fritters. Keep these hot.
5. Grill the sole. Cream the potatoes.
6. Keep sole and potatoes warm and dish up soup.

Oxtail Soup

1 small oxtail. 1 small turnip. 2 medium carrots. 1 medium onion. 3 pints stock or water. 2 oz flour. 2 oz lard or dripping. Salt, pepper. As many mixed herbs as possible, thyme, marjoram, bay leaf, parsley (a small sprig of each).

The butcher will cut the tail into neat joints for you. Soak this for an hour or so. Heat the lard in a pan and fry the sliced vegetables for about 5 minutes. Add the stock, oxtail, herbs (tied in a muslin bag) and simmer gently (with the lid on the pan) for about 3 hours. Blend the flour with a teacup cold stock or water and stir this into the soup. Bring to the boil and cook for about 10 minutes. Remove the bag of herbs. Your soup is a very substantial course, for it includes all the meat. It can be served as a meat dish if wished. To make a finer soup let the above mixture get quite cold. If you don't like foods too fatty remove the fat from the top. Take out the pieces of oxtail and cut the meat from the bones; it will come away in small pieces. Return to the soup and re-heat.

Grilled Sole

Keep the sole whole, but ask the fishmonger to remove the dark skin. Have the grill hot, then lay the sole on the grid of the grill pan, sprinkling with a little salt, pepper, a squeeze of lemon juice, and spreading at least ½ oz, but preferably 2 oz, butter over the top. Cook steadily for about 4 minutes. Turn and re-season the other side, adding more butter. Cook in the same way for about 4 minutes. Some of the butter will drip into grill pan – pour this over the fish when cooked. Put onto very hot dish and keep hot. Try not to keep too long for the fish will be dry.

Apple Fritters

For the batter. *4 oz flour (with plain flour use 1 teaspoonful baking powder). 2 eggs. ¼ pint milk.*

OMELETS

22. When omelet is set on one side, loosen edges and tip pan from side to side to allow liquid egg to flow underneath. 23. When whole omelet is set, slip palette knife beneath it and fold away from handle (Page 121)

24

CORNISH PASTIES. Put a good pile of meat, potato and onion in the centre of each round of pastry, brush edges of pastry with water, then bring them together in the centre (Page 127)

SCOTCH EGGS. Wrap each hard-boiled egg in a square of sausage meat to form shapes as on right (Page 134)

25

26

A complete meal on the grill Steamed pudding, potatoes and peas are cooked on top of grill, cutlets and kidneys on the grid, tomatoes and mushrooms in grill pan (Page 189)

27

Open sandwiches look bright and attractive and are very easy to make. The 'fillings' can be spread on biscuits, halves of bridge rolls, bread and butter, or toast (Page 197)

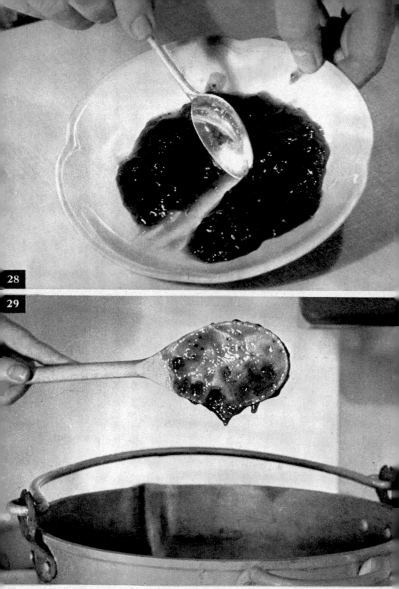

TESTING JAM

28. Allow a little of the jam to cool on a saucer. It has reached setting point i[f] wrinkles slightly and a skin forms when the saucer is tilted or the jam is touch[ed] with a spoon. 29. Allow to cool on wooden spoon, then hold over pan. Jam sho[uld] 'flake' on edge of spoon like this. If it runs off it is not ready (Page 2[6])

Either pan of deep fat or 3 oz lard or dripping. 3 large cooking apples. 1 tablespoonful flour.

Make the batter according to the directions on p 86 for Yorkshire Pudding, but this will be much thicker.

There is, however, a better way of making batter for fritters; make the batter with the egg yolks only. Just before dipping the fruit in *fold*[1] in the stiffly beaten egg whites. This gives a much lighter result. Peel and core the apples, and cut into rounds about one-third inch thick. Dip each slice in flour, for this makes the batter stick to the fruit. Dip into the batter, just before frying. Have the fat very hot (*see* p 117), then drop in the fritters. The moment they go into the fat you must reduce the heat, otherwise you'll burn the outside by the time the apple is cooked. They must take about 6–7 minutes to become golden brown and crisp, or they will not be done through. Drain on crumpled tissue paper then remove to hot dish. Dust with castor sugar just before serving.

Variations

Banana. Cut the bananas into halves lengthways. Banana Fritters are delicious served with apricot jam or sprinkled with sugar and lemon juice.

Pear. Use dessert pears, halved and cored.

Plum. Use large fruit if possible. Cut into halves, and remove the stones. Put the two halves together again and dip in batter; they can be sandwiched together with a little cream cheese for an unusual and delicious sweet.

Dried Fruits. Dried apricots, bananas, peaches, and prunes can be soaked and then dipped in batter.

Light Lunch or Supper
Meat Balls
Potato Hash
Sliced Beetroot

[1] *See* p 49.

Meat Balls

1 tablespoonful flour. Dripping or lard. 6 oz minced cooked meat. (poultry could be used instead). 2 rashers of bacon. 1 teacup breadcrumbs. 1 egg. Salt, pepper. ½ teaspoonful Worcester sauce. 1 teaspoonful chopped parsley. 1 teaspoonful chopped chives.

Cut the bacon into tiny pieces, as small as you can, and fry these until crisp. Mix with all the other ingredients, then form into balls the size of a walnut, roll in flour, and fry in about 2 oz hot lard or dripping. Arrange on hot potato hash.

Potato Hash

Approximately ½ oz lard or dripping. ½ teacup left-over gravy. About ¾ lb left-over potatoes.

Mash the potatoes with the gravy. Heat the lard or dripping and spread the potato over the pan. Turn the heat very low and cook for about 10 minutes, until you have a lovely brown crust at the bottom. Turn the pan upside down over a hot plate or dish, so that the potato cake drops out, and keep this hot while you cook the meat balls.

Sliced Beetroot

Slice the beetroot thinly, pour over a little malt vinegar, and add salt and pepper to taste. If you are fond of the flavour of onion then add a very little grated onion to the beetroot.

Christmas Catering

Do not let the thought of planning the Christmas dinner alarm you, for much can be done beforehand – more in fact than for an ordinary meal. You won't, therefore, find it difficult to prepare the meal and entertain your guests at Christmas-time.

Directions for making stuffings, etc, to accompany the poultry you have chosen are given on p 180. Stuffings, like several other parts of the meal, can be prepared overnight.

Here is the plan of work and the menu for a dinner with turkey as the main dish.

Christmas Dinner
Melon
Roast Turkey   Veal Stuffing[1]   *Forcemeat Stuffing*
Roast Potatoes   Brussels Sprouts
Roast Sausages   Bread Sauce
Mince Pies
Christmas Pudding   Sherry Custard
Fresh Fruit

Some weeks before Christmas you can make the Christmas pudding and the mincemeat, for both of these keep perfectly, if correctly made and stored (recipes on p 181 and p 182).

PLAN OF WORK

CHRISTMAS EVE

1. Prepare the vegetables. Keep sprouts in colander and potatoes in a saucepan of cold water.
2. Make the mince pies and cook these, so that they only require warming.
3. Make the stuffings.
4. Prepare the breadcrumbs for the bread sauce (*see* p 55) and put these, together with the peeled onion, in a paper bag so that they do not dry. Simmer giblets, then strain off the stock for the gravy.

CHRISTMAS DAY

1. Stuff the turkey. Put into oven which has been pre-heated. Baste about three times during cooking (*see* p 48).
2. Put Christmas pudding on to steam.
3. Make bread sauce, and let this infuse as suggested on p 140.
4. Have gravy ready in small saucepan, and custard mixed in a basin, ready to thicken.
5. 1 hour before turkey is done put potatoes in hot fat round the bird (*see* p 181).
6. ¾ hour before turkey is cooked put sausages in hot fat round the bird (*see* p 181).

[1] *See* p 141.

7. Cook sprouts, then put on bread sauce to heat through.
8. Put bread sauce in hot sauceboat, and keep this hot either on a plate over boiling water or in the coolest part of the oven.
9. Turn Christmas pudding out of basin onto hot plate, and stand this over the pan of boiling water covered with the basin.
10. Make gravy, make custard sauce. Put both into sauceboats or dishes and keep hot in the oven.
11. Dish up turkey, potatoes, and sprouts on hot dishes.
12. If you are having melon first put these into the oven, now turned *very low*, together with the mince pies, while you enjoy the melon.

Melon

Cut the melon into thick slices – do not remove the peel. Put on individual plates and have a small dish of castor sugar and a small dish of ground ginger on the table.

Roast Turkey

For a bird about 12 lb you will need about three times the quantity of stuffing in recipe on p 141. Lift the large flap of skin at the neck end and press the stuffing under this (*see* directions under chicken, p 141). There is no need to have more than one kind of stuffing, but many people enjoy two types, so at the other end of the bird you can use a forcemeat stuffing (recipe below). To stop this falling right inside the carcass and being difficult to get out as you carve the bird, put a large piece of bread in first.

Having stuffed the turkey put it into the roasting tin – covering the breast with rashers of fat bacon, or paper liberally greased with lard or dripping. Put into the roasting tin with 6–8 oz dripping. Cook for the first 45 minutes in a hot oven, Mark 6–7 or 425–450 deg. F., then for the rest of the time in a moderate oven, Mark 4–5 or 350–375 deg. F. Pour the hot fat over the bird, ie, baste it, about three times during cooking to keep the flesh moist.

Forcemeat Stuffing

1 lb sausage or sausage meat. The cooked meat from the giblets. 1 tablespoonful chopped parsley. Good pinch salt and pepper.

This makes enough stuffing for a 12 lb bird. Mince or chop the giblets finely. Mix all the ingredients well together. Remove the skin from the sausages.

Roast Sausages

Prick the sausages and if there is room in the tin round the turkey, arrange them in this. If not put into a little hot fat in another baking tin. Allow about 35–45 minutes according to size.

Roast Potatoes

Either put in hot fat round the turkey, or in hot fat in a separate dish. As the oven is a little lower than usual allow a good hour.

Bread Sauce

Follow recipe on p 140, but remember this is only enough for 4 people. If you double quantities you still need only 1 onion.

Mince Pies
To make about 12

FOR THE SHORT-CRUST PASTRY. *8 oz flour (preferably plain). 4 oz fat (preferably 2 oz margarine, 2 oz lard). Pinch salt. Cold water to mix (see p 65).*

or you could use flaky pastry – using 8 oz flour, etc (see p 156).

FOR THE MINCEMEAT. *½ lb mixed dried fruit (4 oz currants, 2 oz sultanas, 2 oz raisins). 2 oz candied peel. 2 oz grated raw apple. 2 oz sugar, preferably brown. 2 oz shredded suet. 2 oz blanched chopped almonds. Grated rind and juice of ½ lemon. 1 dessert-spoonful golden syrup or black treacle. ½ teaspoonful mixed spice. ½ teaspoonful cinnamon. Grating of nutmeg. 2 tablespoon-fuls brandy, rum, whisky, or orange juice.*

Wash and dry the fruit very thoroughly (see p 23). Mix all the ingredients thoroughly together. If using brandy, rum, or whisky you can rely upon the mincemeat keeping for many months, provided you store it in covered jars in a cool place. It is therefore worthwhile making a larger quantity than you need for Christmas. If using orange juice it is not wise to rely upon the mincemeat keeping longer than several weeks.

Cut the pastry into 24 rounds. Line 12 patty tins with the pastry, then put mincemeat into the centre of each; put the remaining rounds of pastry on top, lightly pinching the top and bottom rounds together. Bake in the centre of a hot oven, Mark 6–7 or 425–450 deg. F., for about 20 minutes. Reduce heat after 10 minutes if necessary. Dust with sugar before serving.

Christmas Pudding

To make one large pudding enough for
8–10 people, or two smaller ones

Your Christmas pudding will be improved in flavour if you make it at least six to eight weeks before Christmas. You may, however, like to keep it for a whole year before you use it, when the flavour will be richer still.

1 lb mixed dried fruit (4 oz currants, 4 oz sultanas, and 8 oz raisins). 4 oz shredded suet. 4 oz sugar, preferably brown. 4 oz breadcrumbs (see p 55). 2 oz flour (either plain or self-raising). 1 tablespoonful black treacle. Grated rind and juice of 1 lemon. Grated carrot (small). Grated apple (small). 2 eggs. 4 oz candied peel. 4 oz chopped blanched almonds. ¼ pint milk, stout, beer, whisky, or rum. 1 teaspoonful spice. ½ teaspoonful cinnamon. Grating of nutmeg. Wash and peel the carrot. Peel and core the apple.

Put dry ingredients into a large bowl. Stir in carrot, apple, lemon and treacle, and gradually add the eggs and milk or ale. Let the mixture stand in the bowl overnight, then transfer to required number of well-greased basins. Cover with greased paper very thoroughly (*see* p 78) and steam for about 8 hours if making one large pudding or 5–6 hours for smaller puddings. You cannot overcook a Christmas pudding; the longer you cook it the better the flavour and the more certain you are that it will keep. When the pudding is cooked take off the wet paper and cover with fresh paper. Store in a cool dry place. On Christmas morning steam again for 2–4 hours.

Sherry Custard

Make a custard sauce with custard powder in the usual manner, but just before serving stir in a good tablespoonful sherry to each ½ pint custard.

BOXING DAY

Most people are quite happy to have a cold meal on Boxing Day. Here, therefore, is an attractive cold menu.

Tomato Soup
Cold Turkey and Tongue
Potato Salad[1]   Green Salad[2]
Trifle[3]   Fresh Fruit Jelly[4]
Cheese and Biscuits

PLAN OF WORK

1. Make the trifle and jelly early in the day so that they are cold and set. To make a jelly quickly, use only half the quantity of very hot water, then stir in cold water.
2. Prepare the vegetables first and make the salads.
3. Make the tomato soup.
4. Arrange meat on plates or dish, attractively garnished.
5. Make a cheese plate.
6. Dish up soup.

Tomato Soup

2 rashers of bacon. 1 small onion. 1 lb tomatoes. 2 bay leaves. ½ pint water. Salt, pepper, ¼ teaspoonful paprika pepper. Good pinch sugar. 1 oz margarine.

This makes enough for 4 people. Heat the margarine, then fry the thinly sliced onion. Chop the bacon well and fry this, then add halved tomatoes, and all other ingredients. Simmer gently until very soft, rub through a sieve then re-heat. Serve croûtons of fried bread with the soup. To make these cut the bread into tiny squares about the size of your little finger-nail. Fry in about 1 or 2 oz shallow fat until golden brown (*see* Fried Bread, p 96). Drain well and put on a plate so that people can help themselves.

Cheese and Biscuits

When entertaining try to have a good variety of cheeses, say, three of different types: a good British cheese – Cheddar or Cheshire; a soft cream cheese; an imported cheese such as Gruyère or Camembert (*see* p 26).

Arrange the cheeses on a large plate with the biscuits round

[1] *See* p 67.   [2] *See* p 68.   [3] *See* p 136.   [4] *See* p 110.

and neat pats of butter in a separate dish. Garnish with lettuce, watercress, or parsley.

Boiled Ox Tongue

You may always prefer to buy sliced cooked tongue, but if you have the opportunity to buy a whole tongue at the butcher's, this is the way to cook it:

The most useful and usual tongue your butcher will sell you will be an ox tongue, weighing probably about 5 lb. This will have been salted, so soak for several hours in cold water. Put into a large pan of cold water, adding a few bay leaves but no more salt. Simmer gently, allowing about 40 minutes to each lb. Remove the tongue from the liquid, cool the tongue slightly, then pull off the thick skin. Roll the tongue round to fit into a cake tin or a saucepan; it must be a fairly tight fit, so that you get a neat round. Boil the liquid quickly with the lid off the pan until you have about ½ pint. Pour this over the tongue. Put a plate on top with a weight and leave overnight. The next day dip the tongue in warm water to loosen the sides and turn out on to a dish. Any left over can be braised with vegetables (as for hearts, p 168), but since it is already cooked allow only about 40 minutes cooking time.

Lambs' Tongues

You may be able to purchase the smaller lambs' tongues, each one weighing about 8–12 oz. These are soaked and cooked in the same way, but need about 1½ hours to get them quite tender.

Using Special Parts of Your Cooker

Here are some ideas for saving fuel and time by using only one part of your cooker for a complete meal.

TO COOK A COMPLETE MEAL IN THE OVEN

Hot Pot. (*See* p 153.)

Braised Meat. STEAK (*see* p 185); or CHOPS (*see* p 185); or HEARTS (*see* p 168); or CHICKEN CASSEROLE (*see* p 195).

Vegetables. BAKED JACKET POTATOES (*see* p 88); OVEN-BAKED ROOT VEGETABLES (*see* p 185).

Slow-cooking puddings. RICE PUDDING (*see* p 122); EGG CUSTARDS (*see* p 127).

Braised Steak and Onions

2 oz lard. 1 oz flour. 1 pint stock or water, flavoured with a little Marmite or Bovril. 4 carrots. 3 large onions. Approximately 1 lb stewing steak. Salt, pepper, pinch dry mustard. Good pinch mixed herbs. Cut the steak into neat fingers.

Heat the lard in the saucepan first, then fry the sliced onions and steak until a pale golden colour. Lift into the casserole. Blend the flour with the remaining fat and cook for several minutes, then gradually stir in the cold stock or flavoured water. Bring to the boil and cook until thickened. Season well, adding the herbs and sliced carrots. Pour over the beef and onions. Put the lid on the casserole and cook in a slow oven, Mark 2 or 275–300 deg. F., for 2½–3 hours.

Braised Chops

Follow the same directions as for Steak, but use sliced tomatoes instead of carrots.

Oven-baked Vegetables

Cut root vegetables into slices. If you wish them to cook for the same length of time as the meat casserole then you must have large pieces – halved potatoes, halved carrots. Put into a casserole, add seasoning, half a gill of water – or enough to cover the bottom of the casserole – and about 1 oz margarine. Put a lid or greased paper on the dish and cook in the coolest part of the oven. If cooking for a shorter time then the vegetables may be cut into thin slices.

TO COOK A COMPLETE MEAL IN A STEAMER

As already mentioned on p 16, a two- or three-tier steamer is an excellent investment, for you can have a variety of foods and as with oven cooking the meal can be left more or less unattended if you make sure the heat is turned low enough to prevent the water boiling dry.

Steak and Kidney pudding (*see* p 71); or

Bacon and Rabbit pudding (*see* below); or

Bacon and Onion (or Mushroom) pudding (*see* p 187); or

Stewed Steak (*see* p 172); or

Steamed Chicken (*see* p 105).

Root vegetables (*see* p 187).

Custard (*see* p 127); or

Rice pudding (*see* p 187); or

Steamed Sponge pudding (*see* p 78); or

Dried Fruits (*see* p 187); or

Fresh Fruits (*see* p 188).

If you have only two tiers it may be possible to arrange the vegetables round the basin containing the pudding or sweet, but be careful not to pack so tightly that you prevent the circulation of steam.

Bacon and Rabbit Pudding

Suet Crust.[1]

For the filling: *½ large or 1 small rabbit. 3 rashers of bacon. 1 tablespoonful flour. ½ teaspoonful salt. Good pinch pepper. Good pinch sage. ¾ pint water.*

First soak the rabbit (*see* p 76), then with a sharp knife cut all the meat from the bones. Put the bones with the water, salt, and pepper into a saucepan and simmer gently for about ¾ hour. Strain off the stock. Line the basin with suet crust (as for Steak and Kidney pudding, *see* p 71). Roll the pieces of rabbit in the flour, mixed with good pinch salt, pepper, and the sage. Put alternate layers of rabbit and bacon into suet crust, cover with ¼ pint rabbit stock and the rest of the suet pastry. Cook as for steak and kidney pudding. When you serve the pudding heat the rest of the rabbit stock, and use to fill up the basin.

[1] *See* p 71.

Bacon and Onion (or Mushroom) Pudding

Suet Crust.[1]

For the filling: ½ *lb bacon. 4–8 oz onions or mushrooms. Good pinch salt, pepper. ¼ pint stock or water.*

Line the basin with suet crust (*see* p 71). Chop the bacon into pieces, and the onions or mushrooms, peeled, into slices. Sprinkle with salt and pepper and add the stock. Cook in the same way as the steak and kidney pudding, but this will need only just over 2 hours' cooking.

Steamed Vegetables

The modern method of cooking vegetables is in the minimum amount of water, and as quickly as possible (*see* p 38). Since steaming is not particularly quick it is not the best method, but on occasions it does not hurt to steam root vegetables – including potatoes – for the flavour is good. Do not try to cook green vegetables in this way.

Slice the vegetables or cut potatoes into halves. Put in the steamer, sprinkling with salt very *lightly*, since your seasoning is more concentrated, and cook for about 45–60 minutes according to size of the vegetables and the speed with which the water in the saucepan is allowed to boil.

Rice Pudding Cooked in a Steamer

Use the recipe on p 122, but put the rice and other ingredients into a basin instead of a pie dish. Allow about 2 hours steady steaming. The rice will have an excellent flavour, but no brown skin will form on the top. If you particularly like this you could put the basin (or transfer the pudding to a pie dish) under a hot grill for a few minutes.

Dried Fruits Cooked in a Steamer

The long slow cooking in a basin standing in a steamer is ideal for dried fruits.

Apples. Soak the fruit overnight in cold water. Use enough water to cover all the dried fruit. The next day add the rind and juice of a lemon, a little sugar or golden syrup, and cook gently for

[1] *See* p 71.

about 2 hours in a basin in a steamer. The rind should be in fairly large pieces so that it can be easily removed when the fruit is soft.

Apricots. As apples, using lemon rind and juice if wished.

Figs. Soak the figs overnight, using enough cold water to cover. Add just a little sugar and simmer the figs for about 1½–2 hours in a basin standing in the steamer. If you are particularly fond of the flavour of coffee you may like to soak and cook the figs in a mixture of coffee and water. This gives a delicious flavour.

Peaches. As apples and apricots.

Prunes. Soak and cook as apples, adding a little sugar or golden syrup. For a change use weak tea instead of water to soak and cook the prunes; this gives a most unusual flavour and a richness to the fruit.

If not cooked in a steamer dried fruits should either be cooked in a casserole or simmered very slowly in a saucepan. If using a casserole, keep the lid on, cook in a very low oven, Mark 1–2 or 275–300 deg. F., for approximately the same time as for steaming – apples do not take quite so long. If simmered in a saucepan allow 1–1¼ hours.

Dried Fruit Cooked in a Pressure Cooker

Pressure cookers are admirable for dried fruits, since they shorten cooking time without spoiling the fruit. Instructions are given by the manufacturers of pressure cookers on correct times – approximately 8–10 minutes at 15 lb pressure.

Fresh Fruits Cooked in a Steamer

This is an excellent method of cooking fruit, since one can use little water (or no water in the case of rhubarb) without fear of the fruit burning. Allow about twice as long as when you simmer gently in a saucepan. Put fruit, sugar, and water in a basin.

TO COOK A COMPLETE MEAL ON THE GRILL

Most modern cookers have an excellent grill, particularly gas and electric models. With the latter you are often advised to cook a quite ambitious meal on just the one plate, known as the griller-boiler, and it is quite possible to keep three saucepans boiling while you cook underneath (*see* Pl 26).

The following assumes you can cook at least two pans of food above the grill while cooking underneath, and makes full use of both the grill pan and the grid.

Meal 1. ON TOP OF THE GRILL: *Steamed puddings* (*see* p 77). *Mashed potatoes* (*see* p 72).
ON THE GRID: *Steak or mixed grill* (*see* p 190).
IN THE GRILL PAN: *Tomatoes. Mushrooms.*

Meal 2. ON TOP OF THE GRILL: *New potatoes* (*see* Vegetable table, p 40). *Stewed fruit* (*see* p 122). *Sausages.*[1]
ON THE GRID: *Chops or cutlets* (*see* p 143). *Sausages.*[1]
IN THE GRILL PAN: *Tomatoes.*

Meal 3. ON TOP OF THE GRILL: *Poor Knight's Fritters* (*see* p 191).
ON THE GRID: *Fish* (*see* p 128).
IN THE GRILL PAN: *Tomatoes. Potato Cakes* (*see* p 104).

Meal 1

PLAN OF WORK

1. Put on the water for the potatoes. Since it is too early to start grilling the steak you will be well advised to start the potatoes on a boiling ring or hotplate. Make the puddings.
2. Light the grill, and while heating boil the water for the puddings.
3. Put the puddings into the steamer. Transfer the potato saucepan to the top of the grill.
4. Put the prepared mushrooms (*see* p 150) and halved tomatoes in the grill pan. Sprinkle them with salt and pepper and add a little margarine.
5. Put the steak under grill and cook as instructed.
6. Dish up potatoes, mash, and keep warm.
7. Dish up steak, etc. Turn out grill, for the water will keep hot enough to keep puddings warm with heat left in grill.

[1] Prick and cook as chops.

189

Grilled Steak

Use either a rump steak, allowing about 1¼ lb for a good helping for 3–4 people, or ask the butcher for 4 fillet steaks (about 4–6 oz each).

TO ENSURE TENDERNESS bang the pieces of steak with your rolling pin before cooking. This softens the fibres of the meat.

Have the grill very hot. Brush the top of the steak with a little margarine or butter, putting this on very thinly, and add a sprinkling of salt and pepper. Put the steak on the grid and stand this in the grill pan, putting tomatoes and mushrooms underneath. Season. Grill quickly for about 4 minutes – or up to 6 minutes if you wish the outside very brown and crisp. Turn over and grill for the same length of time on the other side. The steak is now well cooked on the outside, but rather raw in the middle, and most people like it this way. If, however, you wish it well cooked then lower the heat and allow about a further 5 minutes.

Mixed Grill

Either buy smaller pieces of steak or a cutlet or chop instead of steak (*see* p 143 for cooking chops), and have one or two sausages and a rasher of bacon for each person. Prick the sausages and put them on the grid with the steak or chops. When cooked dish onto hot plate, put the bacon on the grid, and cook for 2 or 3 minutes.

Small Steamed Puddings

Follow the directions in pudding recipes (pp 77 or 78). Grease and flour dariole moulds and half-fill with the pudding mixture, putting jam or syrup at the bottom if desired. Cover the tops as for a basin, with greased greaseproof paper. Either stand them in a covered steamer over a pan of boiling water or in a saucepan with enough boiling water to come halfway up the tins. Make sure the water doesn't come too high, or it will boil into the puddings and spoil them. Cook for a good 15–20 minutes.

Meal 2

PLAN OF WORK

1. Put on water for the potatoes, on a separate ring or hotplate since it is not time to start the grill. Commence cooking potatoes.

2. Light grill, transfer potatoes to top, and put over the pan of fruit to be cooked.
3. Put the tomatoes in the grill pan, sprinkle with salt and pepper, and put a little margarine on top.
4. Stand the chops and sausages on the grid over the pan, and cook as directed (p 143).
5. Dish up first course and turn out grill, for the heat retained will keep fruit sufficiently hot.

Meal 3

1. Make the potato cakes (*see* p 104). Put an ounce of margarine or lard into grill pan and place this under the grill when you first light it so that it can get very hot. At the end of about 2–3 minutes when the fat is hot put in the potato cakes, and the halved seasoned tomatoes.
2. Stand the fish on top of the grid and cook as directed (p 128).
3. While the fish is cooking start to cook the Poor Knight's Fritters (*see* below).
4. Dish up fritters and keep hot.
5. Dish up fish and tomatoes, keep hot while you brown the tops of the potato cakes under the grill by removing the grid and bringing the grill pan as high as possible for about 2 minutes.

Poor Knight's Fritters

8 slices of bread and butter. 1 egg. 2 tablespoonfuls jam (approx.).
½ teacup milk. 1 tablespoonful sugar. 2 oz lard or butter.

Spread four of the slices of bread and butter with jam and cover with the rest of the bread and butter. Cut into neat fingers. Beat the egg well, mix with the milk. Pour this onto a deep plate and dip the fingers into this. When the lard or butter is really hot fry on either side until crisp and brown (exactly as fried bread, p 96). Drain with a fish slice onto a hot plate, dust with the sugar, and keep hot until the first course has been eaten.

Dinner Parties

Having friends to dinner need not be an ordeal if you plan the meal carefully, so that you have no last-minute preparations that cause you to disappear into the kitchen for long intervals when you should be entertaining your guests. Try, therefore, to choose those dishes that need the minimum of attention, yet look suitable for a special occasion.

Throughout this book I have given menus for typical family meals, which would be admirable for your guests as well if carefully served and garnished. If I were you I should always have a dish you've made several times before, so that you have a good idea of how long it takes you and just how easy or difficult it is to cook. If, however, you want a rather special menu here are two suggestions:

FOR SUMMER

Asparagus with Melted Butter
Cold Roast Duck
Sage and Onion Stuffing[1]   Orange Salad
New Potatoes[2]
Fresh Fruit Salad[3]   Ice Cream
Cheese Straws[4]
Coffee

PLAN OF WORK

1. Make Cheese Straws the day before and store in an airtight tin. You can arrange them early in the morning or evening; garnish with tiny sprigs of parsley.
2. Cook duck and stuffing early so that it has time to get quite cold.
3. Make fruit salad so that it is really cold.
4. Prepare potatoes and asparagus.
5. Arrange the duck on dish, garnishing with lettuce.
6. Make the Orange Salad.
7. Put on potatoes to cook, then chop parsley as garnish.
8. Put on asparagus to cook.
9. Strain the potatoes and put into hot dish with plenty of margarine so that they do not dry. Cover the dish and keep hot in a very low oven; the parsley should be put on just before you bring them to the table.
10. Strain the asparagus into a hot dish or hot platter and cover gently so that you don't break the heads. Keep hot in a very low oven. At the same time pour the melted butter into a

[1] *See p 64.*   [2] *See Vegetable table, p 40.*   [3] *See p 128.*
[4] *See p 196.*

192

dish, and keep this hot also. Try to get the vegetables dished up before your guests arrive. They will not spoil in the oven if you make sure that it is low enough not to dry them, yet hot enough to keep them steaming – about Mark 1 or 275 deg. F.

11. Bring the asparagus and melted butter to the table.

Asparagus

One medium bunch of asparagus is enough for about 4 people. Using a sharp knife, cut off the bottom of the sticks, leaving about 2 inches of the white part so that they can be held easily. Scrape the white part quite clean with the tip of a knife, then put the heads into cold water to wash them. Take out of the cold water, then tie each person's portion together with cotton – not too tightly, otherwise you break the stalks. If you have a very deep saucepan use this, so that the bundles of asparagus can stand upright. If you can't stand the bunches of asparagus upright in the pan, keep them leaning against the sides, for you must try to prevent the delicate tips being in the water, otherwise they might break off. Bring about 1 pint of water to the boil, adding $\frac{1}{2}$ teaspoonful salt. Put in the asparagus, cover the pan with a lid, and cook for 15–25 minutes, depending on the thickness of the stalks. The asparagus is cooked when the *bottom* green part of the stalks is very soft and tender; you can feel this with the tips of your fingers. Lift out carefully, drain in a colander, and put on a hot dish, untying the string but keeping each portion slightly apart so that it is easy to serve. If wished each portion can be put on hot plates.

Allow about 3 oz butter for 4 people. The melted butter can either be poured over the asparagus just before serving or put on the table so that people can help themselves. Since asparagus is eaten with the fingers, you should put a tiny finger bowl of water by each person's plate. In modern households finger bowls are almost forgotten, so you can use small individual glass dishes, and to give your table an attractive appearance float a tiny flower blossom on top of each bowl of water.

Roast Duck

Stuff the duck as a chicken is stuffed (*see* p 141), using sage and onion stuffing (p 64). A duck is much more fatty, so don't cover

193

with fat, and you'll need no fat in the roasting tin. After the duck has been cooked for ½ hour in a hot oven, Mark 6–7 or 425–450 deg. F., lower the heat to moderate, Mark 4–5 or 350–375 deg. F., for the rest of the cooking time, and gently prick the *skin* only of the duck in several places to allow the fat to come out.

Orange Salad

2 very large or 3 small oranges. ¼ lb watercress. 1 lettuce. French dressing.[1]

Prepare the lettuce and watercress (*see* p 68), and when quite dry arrange on a large flat dish. Peel the oranges, then remove as much white pith as possible. You can do this easily if the oranges are put for about 30 seconds into very hot water. Using a sharp knife cut the oranges into rings, removing any pips. Put these on the lettuce, then sprinkle over a little French dressing. You can include sliced tomatoes as well if you wish.

FOR WINTER

Grapefruit[2]
Chicken Casserole
Duchess Potatoes   Brussels Sprouts[3]
Trifle[4] *Lemon Meringue Pie*[5] *or Caramel Custard*[6]
Cheese and Biscuits[7]
Coffee[8]

Note. Instead of grapefruit you could have a Fish Salad (p 135), or hot soup (pp 82, 89), but the secret of entertaining without fuss is to choose a main course, whether hot or cold, that needs little attention.

PLAN OF WORK

1. Put chicken on to simmer.
2. Prepare sweet, if this has not been done overnight.
3. Prepare and commence cooking chicken casserole.
4. Peel potatoes and sprouts.
5. Get grapefruit ready, put into dishes on the table.
6. Put on potatoes to cook.

[1] *See* p 69.	[2] *See* p 70.	[3] *See* Vegetable table, p 38.
[4] *See* p 136.	[5] *See* p 65.	[6] *See* p 146.
[7] *See* p 183.	[8] *See* p 62.	

7. Dish up potatoes, mash well, and turn into Duchess potatoes, putting into the oven to brown for about 15 minutes.
8. Boil the water, put in sprouts to cook.
9. Dish up sprouts, put into hot covered dish, remembering to cover with an extra amount of margarine to keep them moist. Turn the oven very low to keep hot without over-cooking.
10. Serve grapefruit.

Chicken Casserole

1 boiling fowl. 3 tomatoes. 2 onions. 3 rashers of streaky bacon. 2 hard-boiled eggs (not essential). Salt, pepper. 2 oz margarine. 1 oz flour. 1 pint chicken stock.

Put the chicken into a saucepan, with enough water to half cover, a good pinch salt and pepper, and the giblets. Simmer steadily for 1 hour. (This can always be done overnight.) Remove the chicken from the stock, cool slightly, then cut into neat joints. Use a sharp knife or your kitchen scissors. You should have the following pieces: 2 legs, 2 thighs, 2 wings (plus a good piece of body), the back, four joints from the breast. Measure off a pint of the chicken stock, and keep the rest for soups, etc. Chop the giblets into neat pieces. Heat the margarine in a pan, fry the sliced onions and tomato until tender. Stir in the flour and cook for a few minutes, then gradually add the chicken stock. Bring this to the boil and cook until thickened. Add plenty of seasoning. Arrange the chopped giblets, chopped bacon, and joints of chicken in a casserole. Pour the sauce over. Cover the casserole and bake for 2½ hours in the centre of a very moderate oven, Mark 3 or 325–350 deg. F. Just before serving arrange the sliced hard-boiled eggs on top.

Duchess Potatoes

Cook and mash the potatoes as directions on p 72, then beat in 1 egg to each pound of cooked potatoes. The real Duchess potatoes are piped into tiny shapes, but for the first time or so I would just pile the mixture into a dish, forking into an attractive shape on top. Dot the top with a little margarine (use about 1 oz in all) and bake for about 15 minutes in a very moderate oven to brown the top.

A Buffet Party

This is an excellent choice for a newcomer to cooking, for everything can be prepared before the guests arrive, and there are no last-minute preparations to be made.

Cocktail parties are planned on similar lines, but then all food *must* be very small, for your guests have to hold it in their fingers, so choose things that are easy to manage.

Here are some small savouries suitable for any type of cocktail or buffet party.

Cheese Straws

1½ oz finely grated cheese (preferably Parmesan). ½ oz margarine. 2½ oz flour (preferably plain). A good pinch salt, pepper, cayenne pepper. Yolk of an egg.

Rub the cheese and margarine into the flour. Add the seasoning and mix with the egg.

Roll out thinly, then cut into about 18 tiny fingers. Lift these onto a greased baking tin and bake for 7 minutes in a hot oven, Mark 6–7 or 425–450 deg. F. Cool on tin.

Sausage Rolls

Flaky pastry (see p 156). To 8 oz pastry allow 8 oz sausage meat. Beaten egg yolk.

Roll out pastry very thinly, then cut into long strips about 2 inches wide. Roll the sausage meat into one long thin strip about ½ inch thick. Place this on the strip of pastry, fold over, seal the edges, then cut into tiny rolls – from 1–2½ inches long (1 inch is correct for a cocktail party). Put these on a baking tin, cut two slits on top for the steam to come out (use your kitchen scissors) and brush the top with beaten egg yolk to give a glaze. Bake for about 10–15 minutes in the centre of a hot to very hot oven, Mark 7–8 or 450–475 deg. F.

Cheese Wafers

Sandwich ice-cream wafers together with melted margarine and grated cheese (preferably Parmesan). Put into the oven for a few minutes to melt the cheese. Cut into fingers for a cocktail party.

Have also tiny dishes of cocktail onions, potato crisps, gherkins, and olives, all of which can be purchased in small quantities. More substantial savouries can be made, such as the following:

Asparagus Rolls

Cut very thin slices of brown bread and butter; use fresh bread and remove the crusts. Open a tin of asparagus tips, drain these well, or use cooked asparagus (*see* p 193). Put one tip on each piece of bread and butter, then roll this tightly. Keep under damp cloth until ready.

Ham Rolls

Cut neat pieces of ham about 3 inches by 2 inches. Mix cream cheese with a very little chopped parsley, chopped chutney, chopped gherkins. Spread this over the ham, then roll tightly and put onto fingers of fresh bread and butter.

Mushrooms on Fried Bread

Fry rounds of bread (*see* p 96) then fry whole small mushrooms (*see* p 150). Put the mushrooms on the fried bread and just before the party heat through in the oven.

Open Sandwiches and Sandwich Fillings

Plate 27 shows how interesting open sandwiches can look, for the bright and attractive fillings can be seen. The fillings can be spread on biscuits, toast, halves of bridge rolls, bread and butter, or toast The last-named is the least successful, for with keeping, it tends to soften and become rather limp. Always keep sandwiches, whether the open type or closed variety, under damp cloths until ready to serve, so that they do not dry. Put clean cloths into warm water, then wring out as tightly as you can, and spread over the plates or dishes.

Here are some easy and attractive fillings:

Anchovy Butter. Mix a teaspoonful anchovy essence into 1 oz butter or margarine and beat until soft and smooth. Spread over squares and decorate with rings of sliced stuffed olive. (Both anchovy and olives are obtainable in small bottles.)

Anchovy and Cream Cheese. Open a tin of anchovy fillets. Spread rounds of bread and butter or biscuits with cream cheese, then decorate with the fillets of anchovy.

Bacon. Fry or grill the bacon (*see* p 75) and put on bread and butter while the bacon is still warm. With these sandwiches you would need bread on top. Leave with a weight on top until cold, then cut into neat pieces.

Cheese and Dates. Mix together about 2 oz cream cheese with 2 oz chopped dates (perhaps a few chopped nuts, too). This filling is particularly good with malt bread. Sultanas could be used instead of dates.

Cheese and Egg. Chop a hard-boiled egg and work into 2 oz cream cheese, or 2 oz finely grated cheese. If using the latter moisten with a little mayonnaise.

Fish Spread. Mix enough flaked cooked fish (haddock, salmon – fresh or tinned – white fish, such as cod, halibut, turbot, etc) with a little mayonnaise and seasoning. Spread on fingers of bread and butter or biscuits and decorate with rings of gherkin.

Ham and Watercress. Cream together 2 oz margarine, 2 oz chopped ham, 1 tablespoonful chopped watercress. For an open sandwich garnish with ring of tomato.

Potted Meats and Fish. Potted meats and fish can be made more interesting with additional food or garnishes. Fish pastes should be combined with sliced cucumber, tomato, chopped watercress, mustard and cress, prepared and well dried (*see* p 68). Meat pastes can be used with lettuce, tomato, chutney, or chopped pickles.

Savoury Egg. Heat an ounce of margarine in a saucepan, and fry a sliced tomato (skinned – *see* p 173) and a teaspoonful finely chopped onion. When soft add 2 beaten eggs and salt and pepper. Scramble together (*see* p 81). Cool and use as sandwich filling.

Smoked Salmon. Buy a small quantity of smoked salmon; this is expensive, but if cut wafer thin it goes a long way.

Arrange the sandwiches on plates, or small trays covered with a cloth or paper serviette. The latter are much easier to pass round. Garnish the plates or trays with tiny lettuce leaves, watercress, or halved tomatoes so that the effect is gay and attractive.

In addition to savoury dishes, tiny cakes or biscuits are also a favourite with buffet parties.

Make trifles (recipes on p 136), but put these either into individual dishes or waxed paper containers so that they are easier to serve and handle.

Individual fruit salads (*see* p 128) will also be a great favourite, served perhaps with ice cream. The excellent ice creams on the market will keep beautifully if stored either in the freezing compartment of your refrigerator, or put into large Thermos flasks, or wrapped in several layers of newspaper and stored in the coolest place possible. You should be able to store the ice cream for about 12 hours in your refrigerator, 5–6 in a Thermos, and about 3 hours in newspaper.

Drinks, both soft and alcoholic, should be served from a separate table from the food, for it makes things more straightforward. If you can find someone to be responsible for looking after drinks you will then be able to devote your attention to seeing that your guests are well supplied with food.

Picnic Meals

Most people enjoy a meal served out of doors, especially children, and when the weather is fine a picnic is sure to be popular. Here are some things to remember when you next decide to carry food:

Have plenty of drinks available in Thermos flasks, remembering that these will not only keep hot drinks hot, but will also keep water, lemonade, etc, beautifully cool on the hottest day.

Salads can easily be carried in plastic bags or even small screw-topped jars. (*See* directions for preparing salads on p 68.)

Sandwiches (you'll find suggestions for fillings on p 197) keep much more moist if wrapped first in damp lettuce leaves, then in greaseproof paper or plastic bags or picnic boxes.

Fresh fruit should be well washed before being packed. Small fruit salads can be very easily carried in old ice-cream cartons, provided they have well-fitting lids, small jars, or a wide-necked flask.

Savoury patties are easy to make and carry, and keep rather better than sandwiches.

Bacon and Beef Patties

For the short-crust pastry: *8 oz flour (preferably plain). 4 oz fat (preferably 2 oz margarine, 2 oz lard). Good pinch salt. Water to mix.*

For the filling: *3 rashers streaky bacon. 2 skinned tomatoes (see p 173). About ½ lb cooked minced or chopped beef. 1 egg. 1 large teaspoonful grated onion. 1 teaspoonful mixed herbs, fresh or dried. Seasoning.*

For the herbs you can use all parsley if wished or a mixture of parsley and sage. If using dried herbs have only a small teaspoonful, for they are much stronger when used in cooking. Make the pastry according to directions on p 65, then roll out and cut into 16 rounds. Chop the bacon finely, then mix with all the other ingredients, binding with the egg. Put a good spoonful of the mixture in the middle of 8 of the rounds, brush the edges of the pastry (using your pastry brush) with water, put the other rounds of pastry on top, and seal the edges *very firmly* by pressing hard all round. Put carefully onto baking trays, then make an air hole with scissors or point of a sharp knife in the centre of each. Brush with a very little milk and bake for about 25–30 minutes in the centre of the oven. For the first 10 minutes have a hot oven, Mark 6–7 or 425–450 deg. F., then reduce to moderate, Mark 4–5 or 350–375 deg. F.

Bacon, Egg and Cheese Patties

Use the same method and pastry recipe, but for the filling mix together:

1 teacup grated cheese (Cheddar or mixture of Cheddar and Gorgonzola). 1 egg. 4 rashers of finely chopped streaky bacon. ½ teacup breadcrumbs. Salt, pepper, pinch dry mustard.

In addition to these recipes you will find other suggestions in this book suitable for picnic fare, ie,

Scotch Eggs (p 134).

Rissoles or Durham Cutlets (p 137 and p 79), delicious cold with salad.

Fish Cakes (p 93).

Cornish Pasties (p 126).

Section IV

Simple Jams

Jam-making is not difficult, providing you follow a few basic rules and weigh or measure the ingredients carefully, for fruits vary in the amount of pectin (or natural setting substance) they contain, and you must adjust your sugar accordingly. I have given recipes for the most popular jams and those that are easy to make.

RULES FOR JAM-MAKING

1. Always use fruit that is ripe, but *not* over-ripe, for this will stop the jam from setting and may even cause it to ferment or become mouldy.
2. You can use loaf, preserving, or granulated sugar for all jams.
3. Cook the fruit slowly until quite tender, for this softens skins and extracts the pectin.
4. Stir carefully when the sugar is added until you are sure it is completely dissolved, after which boil rapidly, without stirring, to get the jam to set in the shortest possible time.
5. To ensure that the jam boils rapidly, without boiling over, you *must* have a large saucepan or preserving pan. The jam before boiling should only half fill this.
6. Make sure the jars are dry and hot. They can be heated slowly in a very low oven.
7. Pour most jam into the jars as hot as possible. For marmalade and whole fruit jam you must wait for a short time as directed in the recipes, but don't let the jam become cold in the pan before pouring into pots.

8. Fill jars very full.
9. Put the small waxed circles, bought from a grocer's or stationer's, onto the jam immediately it is put in the pots. Then cover with final paper – when cold.
10. Store the jam in a dry, cool, and preferably dark cupboard.

HOW TO JUDGE SETTING POINT

Mention is made in all jam recipes of boiling until 'setting point' is reached. This can be gauged as follows:

1. After boiling for about 10 minutes put a little of the jam on to a saucer. Allow to cool slightly. Meanwhile, either turn off the heat or move the preserving pan away from it, so that jam doesn't overcook. The 'setting point' has been reached if the jam wrinkles slightly, and a skin appears to form when you either tilt the saucer or push the jam with a spoon (*see* Pl. 28).
2. Instead of this method, you can stir your wooden spoon round in the jam, turn the spoon round carefully to cool the jam that will stick to it, then hold the spoon at right angles to the saucepan. If all the jam runs off, then it is not ready, but if you find the jam falling in a 'flake' on the edge of the spoon, setting point has been reached (*see* Pl. 29).

Apricot Jam

1 lb 2 oz apricots (the 2 oz allows for weight of stones removed). 1 lb sugar (loaf or granulated). Juice of 1 lemon. ¼ teacup water (for very ripe fruit). ½ teacup water (for firm fruit).

Halve the fruit, and take out the stones. Put the fruit, water, and stone kernels into a saucepan. There is no need to use the kernels, but these give a pleasant flavour if you care to crack the stones. Simmer gently until the fruit is soft. Add the sugar, stir carefully over a low heat until quite dissolved, add lemon juice, then boil rapidly without stirring until setting point is reached. Pour into hot jars and cover with waxed circles. When cold put on paper covers. This amount should give you about 1¾ lb jam.

Blackberry and Apple Jam

1¼ lb Bramley or other good cooking apples (weight when peeled and cored). ¾ lb blackberries. 2 lb sugar. ½ teacup water.

203

Cut the apples into slices, then simmer gently with the water until nearly soft. Add the blackberries and continue cooking for about 15 minutes. Stir in the sugar over a low heat until it is quite dissolved then boil rapidly, without stirring until jam is set. Pour into hot jars, etc (as for Apricot Jam). This will give 3½ lb jam.

Blackcurrant Jam

1 lb blackcurrants. ½ pint water. 1¼ lb sugar.

Simmer the blackcurrants with the water until *very soft*; do test the skins carefully. Add the sugar, and proceed as for Apricot Jam (p 203). This will give just over 2 lb jam.

Damson Cheese

1¼ lb damsons. ¼ pint water. 1 lb sugar.

Simmer the damsons and water until the fruit is soft. Rub through a sieve, leaving only the skins and stones behind. Return the fruit to the saucepan, stir in the sugar, and continue as for Apricot Jam (p 203). This will give 1⅔ lb jam.

Gooseberry Jam

1 lb gooseberries, moderately ripe. ½ teacup water. 1 lb sugar.

Top and tail the gooseberries. Simmer the fruit until soft, add the sugar, then proceed as for Apricot Jam (p 203). This will give 1⅔ lb jam.

Greengage and Plum Jam

1 lb 2 oz fruit (this allows for stones). 1 lb sugar.

If the fruit is very hard and you think it will stick to the pan, then use ½ teacup water. Method as for Apricot Jam (p 203), using the kernels for plum jam if wished. This will give 1⅔ lb jam.

Raspberry Jam

1 lb very firm raspberries. 1 lb sugar.

Warm the fruit for a few minutes only, stir in the sugar, then continue as for Apricot Jam (p 203), but testing after 5 minutes. This will give 1⅔ lb jam.

Strawberry Jam

Use the same recipe as for raspberry jam, but stir in the juice of a large lemon when the sugar has dissolved. Cool in pan for 15 minutes, stir, then pour into hot jars, covering in usual way. This will give 1⅔ lb jam.

Redcurrant Jelly

1 lb redcurrants. 1 teacup water. 1 lb sugar, or slightly less.

Redcurrants have so many pips in them that it is not a good fruit for jam, but redcurrant jelly is delicious. Simmer the fruit with the water until a soft pulp. Put through a jelly bag (you buy these from a good ironmonger) or put several thicknesses of fine muslin over your sieve, and allow the fruit juice to drip through. Measure this and to a pint allow 1 lb sugar. Actually you will probably have only about ¾ pint juice, so adjust the sugar accordingly. Stir the sugar into the hot juice, and when dissolved boil rapidly until 'setting point' is reached.

Marmalade

Follow the same rules as for jam. The following makes a delicious marmalade, with plenty of flavour, but not too bitter.

1 lb Seville oranges. 3 pints water. 3 lb sugar. Juice of 1 large or 2 small lemons.

Squeeze out all the juice from the oranges and put this carefully on one side. Either shred the remaining skin, pith, and pulp or put through a coarse mincer. Soak this overnight with the water, then put into a large pan and simmer gently until the peel is so tender you can rub it between your fingers. Stir in the sugar, and when dissolved add the lemon and orange juice and boil rapidly, without stirring, until setting point is reached. Allow the marmalade to stand for 20 minutes, stir to distribute the peel, then pour into hot jars. Put on the waxed circles and when cold cover with paper.

To Bottle Fruit

There are many ways of bottling fruit, but undoubtedly the easiest is to use a deep pan, and this is suitable for all fruits. Pressure cookers have instructions for bottling fruit and vegetables, and you can follow the makers' instructions with confidence, for they have been tested most carefully. You can bottle vegetables *only* in a pressure cooker, otherwise they are unsafe.

Here are the rules for bottling in a deep pan. If you have no pan deep enough to cover the jars, use a pail or bread bin. A proper sterilizer has a rack on which to stand the jars. A thermometer is useful but not essential.

1. You must have proper bottling jars: (*a*) screw-topped; (*b*) clip tops; (*c*) patent tops for jam jars. Old honey jars, etc, will *not* do.
2. The fruit must be perfect as for jam-making.
3. Don't try to cut down on the time for the full time is essential.
4. Store the fruit in a dry, cool, and preferably dark cupboard, for too much light spoils the colour.

TO PREPARE THE FRUIT

Small stone fruit such as cherries, damsons, and small plums need only washing and wiping.

Large stone fruit can be halved and the stones removed.

Apples, pears. Peel, core, and halve or cut into slices. These fruits are inclined to discolour badly, so as you peel them drop into a pan or deep bowl of salted water (1 tablespoonful kitchen salt to a quart of water). Do not wash the fruit before putting it into the jars. Pack into the jars and pour over cold water or syrup as instructed.

Peaches. Remove the skin. Do this by putting the fruit carefully into boiling water for about 30 seconds, pull off skins, and keep in cold water until ready to pack the jars.

Tomatoes. If wished these can be skinned (*see* p 173).

1. Pack prepared fruit into jars. Fill to the top of the jars, then pour over enough cold water or cold syrup to cover. To make the syrup, boil together 2–8 oz sugar to each pint of water until the sugar has dissolved, then allow to cool before using. (The less sugar you use, the less the fruit will rise in the jars; it will also have fewer calories, of course!)

Note. Do not add any water to tomatoes, they are a much better

206

flavour if you either skin or halve them, add a light sprinkling of salt and sugar (approximately ½ teaspoonful of each to 1 lb of tomatoes). Raspberries need just a light sprinkling of sugar and no liquid.

2. Put the rubber bands, lids, and clips or screw bands into position, but always remember to give screw bands a slight turn to loosen (about ¼ inch), for if they grip the glass too tightly this cannot expand and will crack.

3. Put the rack into the sterilizer, or if using an ordinary pan, put a layer of thick paper, old cloth, or a piece of wood at the bottom. Pour in enough cold water to cover the jars, and stand the jars carefully in the container, making sure they don't touch each other or the sides.

4. Take 1½ hours to bring the water in the pan to 175 deg. F. (185 deg. F. for halved fruits, that are packed very tightly) – or 195 deg. F. for pears, peaches, and tomatoes. That means a steady simmer, except for the last-named fruits, when the water should be simmering quite quickly.

5. Keep the water at this temperature for 10 minutes, except for the last-named three fruits, when it should be maintained for 30 minutes.

6. Lift the jars out carefully, one at a time, and stand them on a wooden board to cool. Do not handle the jars while hot, except to tighten the screw bands.

7. After 24 hours, remove the clips or screw bands and see if the lids are quite tight. If they are the jars have sealed and it should be safe to store the fruit. If, however, the lids come off, then the jars are not airtight, and you must sterilize again *for the same length of time*. Before doing this, though, try to find out why the jars have failed to seal. It may be that the lids were slightly chipped, the rubber rings had been used before and perished slightly, or that the water in the pan was not brought to a sufficiently high temperature.

INDEX

210

212

214

Marika Hanbury Tenison
Deep-Freeze Cookery 70p

A truly comprehensive guide, which happily combines the general subject of domestic deep-freezing with a host of delicious recipes, all home-tried and tested. There is firm advice on buying and choosing a deep-freeze and clear instructions on its maintenance. The author suggests how the freezer can be used as a budget saver, but also warns on what *not* to freeze.

There are seasonal menus for special occasions, as well as practical charts and reference tables.

'Valuable advice . . . excellent help . . . what more could a deep-freeze owner want?' IDEAL HOME

'A first-rate A–Z of deep-freeze cookery' SUNDAY EXPRESS

Deep-Freeze Sense 75p

The definitive guide to the sensible and economical use of your deep-freeze. Marika Hanbury Tenison, herself a deep-freeze user for over sixteen years, tells you everything about the practicalities, advantages and pitfalls involved.

There is much useful advice on such aspects as preparation and packaging, costs and economy, buying in bulk and length of freezer life of various foodstuffs. In addition to the delicious recipes in the book, there is a seasonal guide to fresh products.

The Times Cookery Book 95p
Katie Stewart

Carefully chosen from the recipes published in *The Times* over the last few years, and including many new ones, this collection of recipes by Katie Stewart is practical, varied and imaginative. Selected to suit both everyday needs and special occasions, these recipes provide a rich source of new ideas for anyone who enjoys cooking.

New Casserole Treasury 60p
Lousene Rousseau Brunner

This collection of over four hundred delicious casserole recipes comes from many countries, from great chefs and country kitchens. And the ingredients range from truffles and pâté to cabbage and beer.

Although so varied, these recipes all share one great advantage of casserole cookery: much of the preparation can be done in advance. And Mrs Brunner has added to the simplicity of her recipes by the sensible use of convenience foods. Her clear, detailed and precise instructions make these dishes a joy for even the most inexperienced cook to create.

Quick and Easy Chinese Cooking 60p
Kenneth Lo

At last — over two hundred authentic Chinese recipes that are not only quick and easy, but also can be made from ingredients you can buy in any foodstore or supermarket.

From snacks to dinner parties, for two people or ten, these delicious recipes are capable of infinite variety. With this book, Kenneth Lo dispels the mystique of Chinese cooking, and with step by step instructions makes it easy for you and your friends to enjoy a cuisine that is varied, nutritious and extremely tasty.

Theodora FitzGibbon
A Taste of Ireland £1.25

There is a flourishing Irish cookery tradition: Irish recipes are to be
found tucked away in odd corners of magazines and cookery
books, but many of these recipes come from private family papers
which have never before been published. They are accompanied by
a remarkable series of historic photographs.

A Taste of London £1.50

The food of London is as varied as its inhabitants and its history,
and Theodora FitzGibbon has mingled London's history with
many excellent recipes. The superb historic photographs give a
unique and touching insight into the bygone days of London.

A Taste of Scotland £1.25

The range of Scots cooking is wide, which is not surprising when
one considers the influence of Scandinavia and the 'well keipt
ancient alliance, maid betwix Scotland and the realme of France',
which inspires stovies, Lorraine soup, even haggis, not to mention
Mary Stuart's favourite biscuits. The photographs – from between
1845 and 1900 – cast their own poignant spell.

A Taste of Wales 95p

Here are many dishes whose Welsh names are themselves poetry:
Cawl Cymreig, Brithyll â Chig Moch, Pwdin Efa, Teisen Nionod . . .
'Once more Theodora FitzGibbon explores the food of another
country of Britain . . . authentic historical recipes are interleaved
with superb, touching photographs dating from the later years of
the nineteenth century' THE TIMES

A Taste of the West Country £1.25

'What a tasty dish ! Dozens of them and all with regional
connections . . . Somerset braised lamb, clotted cream and syllabub
. . . the recipes for these and many more are presented, each
facing a period photograph' EXETER EXPRESS AND ECHO

Herbs for Health and Cookery 60p
Claire Loewenfeld and Philippa Back

'While herbs have never lost their romantic appeal to the imagination
we have tended to forget their practical uses . . . For those who
would like to be more adventurous in their use and knowledge of
herbs, however, there is no better encyclopaedia on the subject'
THE SCOTSMAN

'If you have a garden, then you should rope off a bit for herb
growing and buy the book immediately' NORTHERN ECHO